For Kenneth Wicks

Very Best Wishes,

(signature)

June 4, 1988

Toronto

THE FILMS
OF OLIVIA
DE HAVILLAND

THE FILMS OF OLIVIA DE HAVILLAND

by ***Tony Thomas***

Foreword by Bette Davis

CITADEL PRESS · Secaucus, N. J.

First edition

Copyright © 1983 by Tony Thomas
All rights reserved
Published by Citadel Press
A division of Lyle Stuart Inc.
120 Enterprise Ave., Secaucus, N.J. 07094

In Canada: Musson Book Company
A division of General Publishing Co. Limited
Don Mills, Ontario

Manufactured in the United States of America by
Halliday Lithograph, West Hanover, Mass.

Designed by Paul Chevannes

Library of Congress Cataloging in Publication Data

Thomas, Tony, 1927–
    The films of Olivia de Havilland.

    1. De Havilland, Olivia. I. Title.
PN2287.D36T46   1983   791.43′028′0924   82-19812
ISBN 0-8065-0805-1

CONTENTS

Acknowledgments

As with the other books I have written in this series, I am indebted to many people for their help. Much of my research was done, as before, in the library of the Academy of Motion Picture Arts and Sciences (Los Angeles), for which I thank Mrs. Terry Roach and her staff, and at the library of The American Film Institute (Beverly Hills), for which I thank Anne Schlosser. In the difficult task of collecting the illustrations I am especially grateful to two friends in England, Rick Dodd and Joyce Sheperdson. In that respect I am also indebted to Joanne Yeck; Robert Knutson, the director of the Special Collections Division of the University of Southern California (Los Angeles); Ron Haver, the director of film programming at the Los Angeles County Museum of Art; Eddie Brandt and Mike Hawks of Saturday Matinee (North Hollywood); Bob Colman of The Hollywood Poster Exchange (Los Angeles); Paula Klaw of Movie Star News (New York); Gunnard Nelson; Basil Courtel; David Chierichetti; Rudy Behlmer; Ted Sennett; Homer Dickens; Trudy McVicker; and The Larry Edmonds Bookshop (Hollywood). And a particular bow to the gracious lady who is the subject of this book. Books of this kind can only be done with help of this kind. I am indeed grateful.

Tony Thomas

Foreword

I have utter admiration for the career of Olivia de Havilland. She had a big hurdle, in the beginning, which I did not have. Physically she was beautiful. Warner Brothers only cared that she was beautiful and therefore cast her, not as an actress, but as a leading lady opposite male stars as their love interest.

In the years that followed, after her Warner contract was over, she overcame her beauty. She gave very outstanding performances as an actress. *To Each His Own, The Snake Pit, The Heiress,* these were the most spectacular.

Olivia is also my friend. One day in the Green Room at Warners, after many of our co-stars were dead, she said, "Wouldn't you know we would still be here?" Olivia is still here, I am still here.

Olivia should be thanked by every actor today. She won the court battle that no contract should ever have to continue more than seven years. Years ago our contracts could have been indefinite. A sort of potential contract for life.

Olivia, this foreword is written with respect and deep affection.

Bette Davis

Olivia de Havilland— the Exceptional Lady

Dick Powell once said that in all his long and varied career in Hollywood he never knew a truly happy actress. He pointed out that neurosis, scandal, discontent, worry, and intrigue mar the route to the movie throne room and that the real star of Beverly Hills is the psychiatrist. There is much to support Powell's views.

A successful film actress cannot be an ordinary woman. It usually takes enormous effort in order to find success and even more of it to remain successful. The rewards of admiration and a seemingly glamorous life are extremely seductive but the price tag is high and the ratio of success to failure is very low indeed. For a woman to do well in the movies she must be aggressive, persistent, and self-sufficient, and she must be willing to forego privacy and sensitivity. This she must do while at the same time appearing to be sensitive, appealing, and truly feminine.

A woman in the movies, especially in Hollywood, has mostly been a kind of second-class citizen. Film making, except for a few recent inroads made by women, is largely a man's business, and yet, ever since cameras started to churn in California, young women have descended on the state hoping to get into the movies. Hollywood is still a community full of women either wanting to be famous or trying to hang on to fame.

Hollywood has never disguised the fact that it is a grinding mill. Occasionally there have been fine films made about the film business itself—*A Star Is Born, Sunset Boulevard, The Bad and the Beautiful, The Big Knife,* and *Whatever Happened to Baby Jane?*—and the light cast on the scene is never a flattering one. When Robert Aldrich was trying to raise the money to make *Baby Jane,* the reaction he received from potential backers when they learned his stars were Bette Davis and Joan Crawford was, "What do you want with those two old broads?" In view of that harsh attitude toward a lifetime of apparent success it is not difficult to understand why Miss Davis gave her autobiography the title *The Lonely Life.*

There are, of course, always exceptions to even the most stringent rules. Sometimes, instead of the desperate pursuit that usually marks success in the movies, a career will be easily and simply handed out. This was the case with Olivia de Havilland. It is difficult to think of another example of a young actress with almost no experience being persuaded to sign a long-term contract with a major studio, being given immediate star billing, and enjoying popularity for years thereafter. From that incredibly easy start came a career that would bring her fame and fortune, and the greatest of professional acclaim, including two Academy Awards.

Despite all the tales of personal grief, turmoil, and conflict, Olivia de Havilland's career has been free of psychiatric aid and salacious conduct. Apart from the failure of her two marriages and an often highly publicized, life-long tiff with sister Joan Fontaine, there has been no scandal in her life. She has not been, as often happens, the victim of unscrupulous managers and promoters. Indeed she has to a large extent charted her own course and she is the only woman in film history to have taken a major studio to court and won a case against them.

Olivia was not quite eighteen when she was signed by Warner Bros. to be one of the stars of their much heralded plunge into culture, the lavish depiction of Shakespeare's *A Midsummer Night's Dream* in 1934. A year later, as Errol Flynn's co-star in *Captain Blood*, she attained stardom and security, as Warners placed her in several pictures every year until 1943, when she rebelled against them and went her own way—to even greater success. Seemingly it was all that a young lady could possibly desire. But looking back on it, Olivia is not at all sure it was the best thing for her to have done:

Playing Puck in the Saratoga Community Theatre production of A Midsummer Night's Dream, *1934*

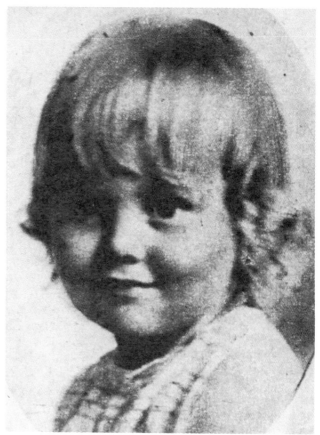

"Film work is much too hard for an eighteen-year-old, your nerves and physical strength are easily exhausted and it does great injury to one emotionally. I think you need the incubation period of going to a university, especially if you are sensitive and have a curious mind. There were many kinds of knowledge that interested me and it was the kind of knowledge that I needed to have and longed for, and which I could get only by a very formal education. I could have saved myself a great deal of pain."

It comes as a shock for her admirers to hear that those early years might have been denied them had she opted for higher education rather than accept the heady offer from Warners. Not to have had her playing Arabella Bishop in *Captain Blood* and Maid Marian in *The Adventures of Robin Hood,* which paved the way for Melanie in *Gone With the Wind,* is disturbing to anyone whose life has been affected by those pictures. But she *did* play those roles and in doing so she gave those movies part of the image that lingers both affectionately and importantly in film history.

Olivia has made her home in Paris since 1956, with frequent trips elsewhere for film making, television appearances, and lecture tours. She did not marry until she was thirty and since then she has clearly attempted to

Ten months old in Tokyo.

Two years old and already a beauty

With Bette Davis in In This Our Life.

With sister Joan

Fifteen

*At sixteen, the secretary of
the Los Gatos Union School
student body*

have a private life as well as a professional one. In the dozen years prior to marriage she was a nose-to-the-grindstone actress, with a personal life that suffered as a consequence. Despite the fact that her great period of acclaim came after the age of thirty and that she has made fewer films since that age than before it, Olivia was determined not to let fame rob her of satisfactions of a more personal nature. Even though her two children are grown, she still opts for home and social life. "I have two lives and I think all really feminine women in this business must have them, no matter how creative they are. I do need the life of imagination, there isn't any question about it. My life would be incomplete if I didn't have it, but I also need the·life of a family and the sort of creative expression that one has though one's children and through one's domestic life, and I have that too. I'm very fortunate but I do need both. I need both of them."

In his autobiography, *My First Hundred Years in Hollywood* (Random House, New York, 1964), Jack L. Warner recalled when he first saw Olivia in 1934: "I saw a girl with big, soft brown eyes, like those in a Keane portrait, and a fresh young beauty that would soon stir a lot of tired old muscles around the film town. She had a voice that was music to my ears. Like a cello, low and virbrant. . . ." Warner would learn in time that the docile, quiet manner was the mere exterior of a young lady of inner strength and unbending determination. Later he described her as having "a brain like a computer concealed behind those fawnlike brown eyes."

The word most often used to describe Olivia is "ladylike." As do few film actresses, she indeed does have the bearing and the manners of a lady, of someone well reared in what is now referred to as "the old school" of decorum. There is a patrician quality about her, as there equally is about her sister, and it is a quality honestly arrived at. Olivia Mary was born in Tokyo on July 1, 1916, and Joan de Beauvoir was born on October 22 of the following year. Both parents were English and lived in Japan because of the father's professional life. He was Walter Augustus de Havilland, a graduate of Cambridge University and a gentleman well aware of class distinctions. He was able to trace his ancestry back several hundred years and could name a long line of aristocratic forebears. As a contemporary cousin he had Sir Peter de Havilland, who would become one of England's foremost aircraft manufacturers.

At the time of his marriage in 1914 to Lillian Ruse, de Havilland was a professor of English at the Imperial University in Tokyo but he gave up that post for the more profitable line of patent attorney. His wife, a native of Reading, Berkshire, had studied at the Royal Academy of Dramatic Art in London but her Victorian parents frowned on any involvement in the theatre, while allowing her to perform in the concert world as a singer. After her marriage at the age of twenty-eight (Walter was then forty-two, with all the earmarks of a born bachelor), Lillian occasionally taught dramatic art, music, and particularly elocution, which was her

In her first days at Warners Olivia sat for the usual cheesecake publicity shots, but the studio soon realized that this would not be her image.

21

forte. Her best pupils were her daughters and it is fair to assume their success has much to do with their mother's teachings.

The de Havilland marriage was never a happy one. Walter appears to have been a rather imperious Englishman, given to long hours spent at chess and indulging in the social life of the British colony. Lillian, imperious in her own right, was a forceful lady who became more and more active in staging dramatic and musical entertainment for the European colony as her married life became less and less interesting to her. In February of 1919 she persuaded her husband, somewhat against his will, to take her and their daughters back to England because the girls needed a better climate than Tokyo. Olivia had developed a bronchial condition and Joan was generally weak. They proceeded across the Pacific to San Francisco but by the time they arrived the girls were in even poorer health. "I had developed a high temperature and when we arrived my mother took me to see Dr. Langley Porter, then a noted specialist in children's ailments, who told her my tonsils were highly inflamed and would have to come out immediately. Out they came. Then my sister went down with pneumonia and mother found herself with two invalids on her

During a break in the making of Captain Blood *Olivia crosses swords with Errol Flynn. Just fooling around, of course.*

With Max Reinhardt at the premiere of his A Midsummer Night's Dream. *The other lady is actress Evelyn Venable, the wife of Hal Mohr, the photographer of the Reinhardt film.*

hands. She was advised by Porter, and others, not to continue the trip to England but to look for a nice spot in the nearby country and rest. She found a community she liked very much—the village of Saratoga, about fifty miles south of San Fancisco. Many people had retired there because it was so beautiful, including quite a few English people, and mother loved it. She decided to settle there and not to go to England at all."

Walter de Havilland arrived at his own decision, which was to leave his wife and daughters in California and return to the Japanese housekeeper who would eventually become his second wife. Lillian did not see him again until 1925, when she returned to Tokyo to divorce him. He did not see his daughters again until they were teenagers and there would be little affection shown to them. Lillian raised the girls strictly and protectively but the fact that Olivia was stronger than the ever-ailing Joan caused sibling rivalry. Olivia was allowed to play almost all the children's games while her sister was restrained and encouraged to do nothing more strenuous than reading. It was Joan who, as a child, called her sister "Livvie," a nickname that was to stick. Sadly this difference in health gave rise to a family expression that would gradually have deep emotional significance—"Livvie can, Joan can't." Fortunately time would prove Joan to be a talent and a celebrity of equal rank, but the schism of the early years would never be completely eradicated.

In her autobiography, *No Bed of Roses*, (William Morrow and Company, Inc., New York, 1978), Joan Fontaine made this comment:

> There has always been great curiosity about the relationship between Olivia and me. From birth we were not encouraged by our parents or nurses to be anything but rivals, and our careers only emphasized the situation. As both Olivia and I can be classified as achievers, our impetus may well be the sibling rivalry that still exists. Perhaps, without it we might never have striven to excel, might have been quite content to be housewives or schoolteachers. I doubt it, however. I felt "different" from my first conscious moments. I think Olivia did, too. As very young children we didn't conform or wish to conform to the usual behavior patterns. We didn't want to be like everybody else. We strove to be individuals, to make our personal mark on whatever we were doing. Only in our clothes did we try to be inconspicuous, wearing the same saddle shoes, the same length dresses as our classmates. To this day we have maintained our own individuality.

Lillian de Havilland's thwarted ambition to be an actress, in addition to her talent as a teacher, naturally led her daughters toward involvement in the arts. Lillian was a devotee of Shakespeare (his *Twelfth Night* was the source of Olivia's name) and the girls were coached in recitations from his plays while still very young. They therefore grew up with elocution as a natural function of life, a fact that would be greatly to their benefit in films. Clarity of diction and a well modulated, mid-Atlantic speech has been a strong factor in their frequent casting as patrician ladies in classic material.

Olivia recalls those early years and the almost Victorian upbringing in a quiet, idyllic California town in the Twenties. "Like many other little girls, at the age of four I took ballet lessons, at five I was taking piano lessons, too, but for neither of these arts did I exhibit any particular affection or aptitude. Instead, my great interest was in the game of 'let's pretend.' In school, 'let's pretend' took the form of a recitation or a play. I can remember in the eighth grade, learning with keenest disappointment that I had not been chosen to play either Hansel or Gretel in the school operetta. I volunteered in other capacities, however, so that the night of the performance found me playing the Mother, the Second Angel, and the Head Witch."

With Basil Rathbone and Una O'Connor, just about to leave Chico, California, after completing location shooting for The Adventures of Robin Hood, *November 1937.*

Olivia's education was gained at the Saratoga Grammar School, the Notre Dame Convent in nearby Belmont, and the Los Gatos Union High School. The lives of both her and Joan were greatly influenced, for better and worse, by their mother's marriage to George Milan Fontaine. A storekeeper in Saratoga, he was brought to the attention of Lillian by her daughters when they were very small and much impressed with his friendly, avuncular manner. It was Olivia who first referred to him, in Japanese, as "Daddy." After Lillian was divorced from Walter, she married Fontaine in 1925. A good provider and a respectable citizen, Fontaine was also a martinet whose severe discipline caused the girls to retreat from him. He was not in favor of them having anything to do with the arts and the theatre, and imposed such an early curfew for them as teenagers that they took to doing their homework by flashlight under their bedclothes. His rulings were so strict that he increased the resolve of the girls to do the very thing he forbid—to become actresses. At the age of sixteen Olivia rebelled and moved out of the house to live with friends. She spent much of that summer of 1932 studying typing, at the behest of Fontaine, but by now she had decided on a career as a teacher, specializing in English and speech.

On the publicity junket for Dodge City, *with Alan Hale, Rosemary Lane, director Michael Curtiz, Bruce Cabot, Priscilla Lane, producer Robert Lord and Errol Flynn*

In high school Olivia appeared in plays and became the secretary of the school dramatic club. She excelled in oratory and field hockey and worked to rid herself of what she claims was an extreme case of shyness. Her success in front of audiences was a great help but she would be troubled by shyness even in her early years as a movie star. Her ability in school plays resulted in the Saratoga Community Theatre offering her the lead in *Alice in Wonderland.* "For the first time I had the magic experience of feeling possessed by the character I was playing. I really felt I was Alice and that when I moved across the stage I was actually moving in Alice's enchanted wonderland. And so for the first time I felt not only pleasure in acting but love for acting as well."

In her final year of school, Olivia supported herself by doing odd jobs and by coaching other students. Her mother's bridge club also donated some money to encourage her to continue with acting. After graduation in 1934 she was offered the role of Puck in the Saratoga Community Theatre production of *A Midsummer Night's Dream,* a choice that would dramatically alter the course of her life. Had it not been for the theatre choosing this particular play she would probably have gone to Mills College, from which she had received a scholarship. But this was the summer that the great Austrian director Max Reinhardt came to California to do his celebrated version of *A Midsummer Night's Dream* at the Hollywood Bowl. Friends at the theatre thought Olivia should have a crack at this and invited Reinhardt's assistant, Felix Weisberger, to see their production and meet Olivia. He invited her to visit him in four weeks' time in Los Angeles and possibly do the understudy for the actress who would play Hermia. By the time she got there, Weisberger had forgotten about her and had assigned Jean Rouverol to be understudy to Gloria Stuart. Somewhat embarrassed, he advised her to stay around for a while. A week before the Reinhardt production was due to open at the Bowl, in mid-September, Jean Rouverol left to take a part in a film and her job was handed to Olivia. "Then my life began to take on the character of a bad but exciting novel. On opening night the real Hermia could not go on. There was no one to take her place but the understudy—and the job was mine. Also like a novel, the reviews the next day were very kind to the understudy and I continued in the role until the engagement was completed."

Reinhardt was highly pleased with her performance and insisted she sign for a four weeks' tour of his *Dream.* Since she did not at this time really want to make a career as an actress and had pursued the Reinhardt play in order to increase her standing as a potential theatre arts teacher, Olivia was in a quandary. She told Reinhardt she first wanted to check with Mills College to ask them to hold open their scholarship and they agreed to do so until the end of the year. Olivia then went on the road with Reinhardt and won so much critical acclaim that it became more and more difficult for her to withstand the blandishments of agents and the advice of Reinhardt that she make acting her profession.

The four weeks' tour of Reinhardt's production was confined to points within California but won so much attention that it was decided to extend it and take it to cities in the east, including St. Louis, Milwaukee, and Chicago. Again Reinhardt insisted on taking Olivia and again she accepted, but this time taking her mother on tour with her. It was during this tour that Reinhardt received word from Warner Bros. that they had decided to go ahead with the plans to make a movie of his version of *Dream.* The primary mover in this decision was the German-born executive producer at the studio, Henry Blanke. He had seen Olivia at the Hollywood Bowl presentation and when Reinhardt mentioned Olivia for the film, Blanke was enthusiastically in favor. He smiles when reminded of this and says, "She was so beautiful it hurt."

Reinhardt talked Olivia into being his film Hermia but she was uncertain about the decision. She had set her mind on going to Mills College and on becoming a teacher, and when Warners explained that in order to appear in the film she would have to sign a long-term contract with them she thought it best to refuse. However, she had not reckoned with Austrian charm. Reinhardt and Blanke, along with composer Erich Korngold and director William Dieterle, who would co-direct *Dream* with Reinhardt, all expressed horror at her talk about not being a part of their picture. The eighteen-year-old could hardly be expected to withstand the persuasiveness of these suave gentlemen. "I signed out of weakness and a sense of responsibility. I went home and cried and cried and cried with the most ghastly feeling of depression. I was sure I had made the wrong decision."

Olivia's depression soon abated once she began work on the film, which was months in production. The usually tough Warner Bros. attitude toward film making, which was one of getting product turned out as quickly and economically as possible, was suspended for this excursion into culture. It was a luxurious debut for Olivia and it was deceptive. Once it was finished she was shunted into routine production and quickly learned that she was part of a hard business and that the studio was a kind of factory. The leisurely schedule of Reinhardt's *Dream* was a dream indeed and culture would seldom raise its non-commercial head at Warners again. She had signed a contract which gave her two hundred dollars a week but she had hedged at putting her name on the usual seven-year agreement. She signed for five years, with options, but on April 14, 1936, she finally agreed to the seven-year plan. By then it was obvious both to the studio and herself that she was star caliber. But within a few years she would be feeling resentful of a contract that seemed more and more a matter of indenture to employers who were not much interested in her capabilities as an actress but only in her attractiveness as a successful picture personality.

While the Reinhardt film was in the process of being edited and scored, Olivia was assigned to play opposite Joe E. Brown in *Alibi Ike*, which was released in June of 1935 and became the first movie in which she was seen. In August the public would see her in James Cagney's *The Irish in Us,* but in neither film could they see anything other than simply a very pretty young girl playing routine heroines. She was dismayed to be given these films, thinking that the prestige of being a Reinhardt player had qualified her for quality pictures, but she soon learned she was a Warner contractee and expected to do as she was told. *A Midsummer Night's Dream* was not released until October and met with mixed reviews and a disappointing response from the public. But by this time Warners had made a decision which would have great impact on Olivia.

Errol Flynn had arrived at the Warner studios in Burbank in January of 1935, following a couple of years on the stage in England and many years of being a roustabout in Australia and the South Seas. When Robert Donat decided not to do *Captain Blood,* Warners took a chance on Flynn and thereby created a star of major proportions. After considering other

actresses, the studio then decided to pair him with Olivia and thereby created one of the most potent teams in movie history. The chemistry between them was of the kind for which film producers pray. Both were beautiful specimens, both had a classy air about them, and both were perfect when placed in costumed stories of historical romance. They looked as if they had been lifted out of the pages of a story book and their appeal to the public was instant. And the actual feeling between them was deeply personal, which clearly affected their screen images. With Flynn it was a matter of love at first sight but as he later admitted, he was gauche in trying to impress her and succeeded mostly in scaring her with his rough humor. Olivia felt as strongly about him but since he was then married to Lili Damita she knew there could only be trouble if she allowed herself to return his advances. "It's a good thing I didn't—he would have ruined my life." Flynn was a highly complex and insecure man, despite his charm and talent. She remembers at their first meeting, when they were testing together for *Captain Blood,* asking him what he most wanted. He replied, "Success." In pursuing success Flynn compromised himself and trod a path that eventually lead to veritable self-destruction.

Shortly after Olivia and her mother set themselves up in an apartment on Franklin Avenue in Hollywood, they were joined by Joan, who had also decided on a career as an actress. In order not to conflict with Olivia she took the name of her step-father, who still did not condone the girls' decision to go into the entertainment business. Lillian on the other hand was supportive of both girls and apparently delighted in being a part of the Hollywood scene. Since George Fontaine did not, it could only lead to separation.

Her refined demeanor and her beautiful diction made Olivia an obvious choice for other Flynn swashbucklers and for such costumed outings as *Anthony Adverse* and *The Great Garrick,* but it tended to limit her in other kinds of films. She was displayed in comedies like *Call it a Day* and *It's Love I'm After,* but they did little to advance her career, partly because she had yet to learn how to handle herself in such material. Warner films were made quickly and the directors seldom spent much time discussing roles with their players. It was a catch-as-catch-can method of learning. With her playing of Maid Marian in the enormously popular *The Adventures of Robin Hood,* Olivia discovered the joys of being seen and admired by millions but it did not reflect in the minds of her employers that she was anything more than a pretty star in their firmament. Jack L. Warner evinced no interest in her desire for more expressive material and a chance to do the kind of parts that were being given to Bette Davis.

If the success of *Robin Hood* led her to expect better treatment at the studio, she was wrong. The assignments were if anything even more routine and with her fifth Flynn picture, *Dodge City,* she verged toward depression and nervous collapse. It was a period in which she was given to constant fits of crying and long days spent at home in bed. She was bored with her work and while making *Dodge City* she claims that she even had trouble remembering her lines. She recalls it as about the lowest point in her career.

Now twenty-two and resolved not to let her career slip away, Olivia went after a role she badly wanted to play. Like almost everyone else in Hollywood she wanted to be involved in David O. Selznick's heralded, upcoming production of *Gone With the Wind.* Unlike almost every other actress she was not interested in the role of Scarlett O'Hara. After reading the book she knew she had to play Melanie Hamilton, that it was a part she thoroughly understood and could bring to life. Sister Joan had been thought of as Melanie but she would consider only Scarlett and suggested to George Cukor, whom Selznick had hired to direct, that Olivia would be a better choice. She was, of course, absolutely right, and Olivia's performance as Melanie would become one of her most famous identifications. The problem was to convince Jack L. Warner that she should do the Selznick film. Warner was not the least inclined to let her leave the lot and he also believed Selznick was heading for disaster with a gigantic

On a date with Burgess Meredith in April 1942. Bruce Cabot in the background.

dud. Olivia got the part by appealing to Warner's wife Ann, who felt that Olivia would be perfect for Melanie. Sabotaged on the home front, Warner had to give in.

Olivia's feelings for Jack Warner were like those of most of his stars, a mixture of affection and resentment. His studio was run with tight control and discipline and all but the biggest names and executives had to clock in and clock out. Warner tended to regard actors as wayward children and he was always suspicious of them, always expecting them to misbehave and cause problems. He also regarded them as employees who should obey his instructions. He seldom showed any interest in anyone's career *per se*. He was interested in turning out a profitable product and much of the success of Warners in the golden era of Hollywood is due to his management, in his ability to hire the right people and the right properties for them. He was also a moral man, perhaps more so than most movie moguls, who was happily married and took a dim view of immoral

During the making of Devotion *in December 1942, Olivia has lunch with her English cousin Geoffrey de Havilland, then an officer in the Royal Air Force, having left his job as a designer with the famous family airplane manufacturing company.*

behavior on the part of his employees. Much as he liked the charming Flynn, with whom he kept up a bantering relationship, Warner had no desire to live like him. Olivia looks back on those years with some nostalgia, despite the restrictions, because the studio had the feeling of a family and because she was sheltered. She felt the difference when she would visit other studios—MGM, for example—where she sensed far more intrigue and lechery.

Her acclaim in the Selznick epic still did not lead Jack Warner to treat Olivia with any more deference than before, and there were still no signs of his promoting her career with better pictures. Instead he gave her third billing in *The Private Lives of Elizabeth and Essex,* which was especially irksome because she was in a Flynn film but not starring opposite him. He loaned her to Sam Goldwyn for *Raffles,* for a limp part any pretty actress could have played, and after she returned to the lot he put her in a feeble comedy called *My Love Came Back.* She fared a little better in Flynn's *Santa Fe Trail,* but she finally took matters into her own hands by ferreting around the studio to find scripts which might offer an interesting part. It was in this fashion that she came across *The Strawberry Blonde.* Warner was astonished when she said she did not want to play the title role; as with *GWTW,* Olivia had spotted the part, that of Amy, she knew she could bring to life. Happily it brought her together again with James Cagney, a man she considers one of the most natural and powerful actors in the history of films. "At one point during a lull on the set I turned to him and asked, 'Jimmy, what *is* acting?' He thought for a moment and replied, 'Well, whatever you say—just mean it.' To me it is *the* statement on acting and it has helped me all my life."

Realizing that she would have to go elsewhere to find the kind of material that would lift her career into greater prestige, Olivia went to Paramount to do *Hold Back the Dawn* with Charles Boyer. It was an excellent part and she brought it off to fine reviews, but again it seemed to make no impression on Jack Warner. He had in fact been tricked into letting her go to Paramount; Warner wanted to borrow Fred MacMurray from them and offered them his list of players. They wanted only Olivia but pretended they didn't so that he wouldn't decide not to let her go. The success of the film finally caused Olivia to do something about her confinement at Warner Bros. Always conservative in her lifestyle she now saved as much of her salary as possible for what she sensed would be rainy days ahead.

Olivia appeared for the eighth and final time with Flynn, playing his wife in the Custer biography *They Died With Their Boots On,* which contains the most effective scenes they ever did together. Then she was Henry Fonda's wife in *The Male Animal* and the girl who lost her husband to Bette Davis in *In This Our Life.* Warner, still not caring very much about what happened to her beyond her value as a name, loaned her to RKO for the limp comedy *Government Girl,* an assignment she accepted only because she did not at this point want to rock the boat. Back at Warners she played *Princess O'Rourke,* one of her few really satisfying jobs under the Warner banner, and then concluded her contract with the unconvincing Bronte biography *Devotion.* Olivia now imagined she was free and clear and set to forge ahead with a career as a free-wheeling actress. A shock was about to upset her plans.

Jack L. Warner was not about to let her leave on her own terms. She may have put in seven years but she had caused, as he predicted at the time of *GWTW,* trouble for him. She had also caused the studio to lose

And with mother Lillian

With sister Joan Fontaine at Joan's Hollywood home in 1942

money by not taking roles in films which had been put into production with the understanding she would be in them. She had often refused scripts but in five instances she had refused to turn up for assignments. Warner trotted out the figures and showed her what not doing her parts in *Saturday's Children, Flight Angels, George Washington Slept Here,* and *The Animal Kingdom* had cost him. He also pointed out that her periods of suspension added up to half a year and that it would be tacked on to the end of her contract. She had another six months to go before she could leave the studio.

Olivia decided to put up a fight. She would not do the additional half year at Warners. In August of 1943 her lawyer, Martin Gang, advised her

With Dick Powell during the Hollywood Bond Cavalcade, which was part of the Third War Loan campaign and toured fifteen cities in September of 1944

35

that he had found a possible loophole in the law that might get her free, a law known as "antipeonage" which stated that employers could not hold an employee longer than for the contracted period, and that the maximum period of employment was seven years. If this meant calendar years and not accumulated time, then they had a case. They took Warner Bros. to court, where the studio tried to paint her as a difficult and temperamental artist. The court ruled in her favor but then Jack L. Warner brought his power to bear and wrote a letter, which he sent to 77 studios and production companies:

Gentlemen:

We wish to bring to your attention the fact that the present contract status between Miss Olivia de Havilland and ourselves is the subject of litigation. Miss de Havilland has brought action against us in the Superior Court of California, case #487, 685. Plaintiff is asking for declaratory relief, asserting that her contract is now unenforceable under California law.

Although you have no doubt seen the newspaper accounts of the commencement of this litigation, we wish to bring to your attention the facts and the nature of the question involved. Miss de Havilland entered into a contract with us for her exclusive services under date April 14, 1936. She was a minor at that time and the contract was to become effective and services were to commence upon approval of the Superior Court, as provided by California law. Such contract actually became effective May 5, 1936. It was the usual form of a fixed basic period with optional extensions for a total of three hundred and sixty-four weeks. All options for extensions were duly and properly exercised by us. Such contract also provided for extensions of current periods and of the term in the event the Artist should fail, neglect or refuse to perform the required services. Such defaults and consequent extensions occurred in approximately five instances, and in addition, under date August 13, 1943, Miss de Havilland further failed and refused to report for duty, as requested, and is consequently now under suspension. It is our position that the obligation of this Artist to render services to us will not expire, either under its terms or under the application of any relevant statute, until twenty-five and one-half weeks after she again resumes the rendition of services to us under said contract, and that until she has so performed her obligations, we are entitled to her exclusive services.

Yours very truly,
Warner Bros. Pictures, Inc.
August 30, 1943.

It was a virtual blacklisting and every person who received it abided by it. As a consequence Olivia did not work in a film studio for the better part of two years. During this period she did a few radio plays, mostly for Lux Radio Theatre, with whom she had always been a favorite player, appeared at a bond rally in Madison Square Garden in New York, and toured with the USO to military bases in the Pacific. In September of 1944 the Appellate Court ruled unanimously in her favor and the following February the Supreme Court decided that there was no longer any reason to retain her case in view of the positive decisions made by the first hearing in August of 1943 and the newer one from the Appellate Court. In short, she had won. Jack L. Warner had lost. It had cost her $13,000 in legal fees but she had the consolation of knowing that she struck an important blow for entertainers in America, that henceforth no one could be held beyond a seven-year agreement and that the ruling would forever be known as the de Havilland Decision.

The decision to fight a top Hollywood studio was the bravest ever attempted by a performing artist. Bette Davis had tried it a few years previously but had lost. In doing it, and particularly in winning, Olivia had

Receiving her Oscar as best actress of 1949, and saying thanks after having been handed it by James Stewart

shown her cohorts that the girl they had always known as gentle and gracious was also a girl of determination and strength. It made a considerable difference to her personal and professional standing. It also required her to prove to Hollywood that she was all she claimed she could be once she was free of Warners. After making a feeble comedy for Paramount, *The Well-Groomed Bride,* she stayed at the studio and in June of 1945 she began work on *To Each His Own.* It was released in March of the following year and resulted in her winning an Oscar. Olivia de Havilland had truly vindicated herself.

Nineteen forty-six was a year of great change for Olivia. She was thirty and the Oscar gave her the prestige she had longed for. Her private life all through the years with Warners had been circumspect. She lived quietly and behaved so decorously that people were somewhat shocked if she smoked a cigarette or danced vigorously at a nightclub. By now Hollywood was beginning to wonder why such a lovely girl, one so highly thought of by everyone, was not married. Olivia had dated a number of famous gentlemen, among them Lew Ayres, James Stewart, Franchot Tone, and Burgess Meredith, but the only man with whom she seemed to fall in love was John Huston. Despite talk of marriage, it never happened. Instead she married a man named Marcus Goodrich, eighteen years older than herself, whom she first met briefly in Washington and then fell in love with when she was in Westport, Connecticut, playing the lead in *What Every Woman Knows* by James M. Barrie. Despite her 1934 resolve to do plays as well as films, this was her first chance to get back to the theatre. The title of the Barrie play proved a little ironic; Olivia did not know, for instance, that Goodrich had been previously married four times, a fact he revealed after their marriage on August 26, 1946. His had been a strange career, as a sailor, journalist, advertising man, and stage manager. In 1941 he had had a success with his novel *Delilah,* but it seems to have been his only distinction.

Goodrich returned to Hollywood with Olivia and appeared to become her unofficial manager. Six years later when she divorced him she revealed that hers had been the family income. He was a man with a bad temper and seemed to be amused by the low popularity he acquired in Hollywood, which he looked upon with disdain. Joan Fontaine took a disliking to him and quipped, "It's too bad that Olivia's husband has had so many wives and only one book," a remark that was picked up by the press and caused the rift between the sisters to greatly worsen. At the Academy Award presentations in which she received her Oscar for *To Each His Own,* Olivia raised a lot of eyebrows when she publicly snubbed her sister, who tried to embrace her. Olivia later explained that she was bitter about Joan's quip and expected an apology which never came. She had warned Joan's press agent and her own that she would not acknowledge her without an apology and she was angered upon coming off stage to see a battery of photographers waiting around Joan to catch the event.

"I thought, 'No. No.' I turned away. I was heard mumbling, 'Why does she do these things when she knows they ruin me?' Nobody took the trouble to find out the story." Five years passed before they spoke to each other again. Olivia refers to that time as "my stuffy English period. I know now I was too demanding."

To Each His Own was the start of a three-year period when Olivia was at the absolute peak of her professional form, revealing a depth of talent that surprised even her closest admirers and attaining the kind of success for which all artists strive. After *To Each His Own* came her playing of twins, one good and one evil, in *The Dark Mirror*, and her remarkable portrait of a mentally ill young woman in *The Snake Pit*. This was followed by *The Heiress* and the winning of a second Oscar for portraying another disturbed young woman, one who emerges from pitiful innocence to bitter maturity. The four films contain her finest work and each is a study of the wide-ranging, complex nature of womankind and the problems that beset women, particularly in their convoluted relationship with men.

In January 1949, Olivia received the New York Film Critics Award for her performance in The Snake Pit, *along with Roberto Rossellini, whose* Paisan *was voted the best foreign film of 1948, and John Huston, whose* The Treasure of the Sierra Madre *brought him the critics' best director award.*

Having made those four films, Olivia made a great change in her lifestyle. Realizing that she had spent all her late teenage years and all the years of her twenties as a constantly working film actress, with one picture after another, she now decided to divide her life between the personal and the professional. She had proved all that needed to be proved as an actress, now she needed to catch up on the life of a wife and mother, and to see more of life outside the confines of Hollywood. By the time she finished *The Heiress* she was in an advanced state of pregnancy and advised by her doctor that she needed immediate, prolonged rest to prepare for her child. On September 27, 1949, she gave birth by Caesarean to her first child, Benjamin.

Olivia's marriage to Goodrich was strained by his resentful manner toward Hollywood and its people. He wrote her speech when she accepted the Oscar for *The Heiress* and she was criticized for behaving in a *grande dame* manner. She said, "Your award for *To Each His Own* I took as an incentive. I have always tried to venture forward. Thank you for your very generous assurance that I have not failed." Later that year, 1950, the Goodrich family moved to New York City, where Olivia began rehearsals on an expansive stage production of Shakespeare's *Romeo and Juliet*, Juliet being the role Olivia had always wanted most to play. The play opened at the Broadhurst Theatre on March 11, 1951, and received the kind of mixed reviews that always seem to greet the appearances of famed movie stars when they venture into the theatre. There were those critics who liked her work, those who felt it was beyond her range and those who could not wait to point out that at thirty-five she was too old to play Juliet. The production lasted for 45 performances and lost money for producer Dwight Deere Wiman. Appearing as Mercutio was the popular English actor Jack Hawkins, who mentioned the production in his autobiography, *Anything for a Quiet Life* (Stein and Day, New York, 1974). He commented on the entire $150,000 production being focussed on her and that she received all director Peter Glenville's attention. "To complicate matters, Olivia was at that time married to an author who, for some reason, made it his job to protect Olivia from press publicity. The result of his very efficient endeavors was that when we were ready to open, the American press was just not interested. This obsessive protection also succeeded in working Olivia into a frightful state of nerves."

Undaunted by the disappointment of her *Romeo and Juliet*, Olivia decided to next try George Bernard Shaw's *Candida* in her resolve to prove herself as a stage actress. She opened at the National Theatre in New York in April of 1952 and delivered the 32 performances for which the production was scheduled. Again the notices were mixed, although they were somewhat kinder than for her Juliet. She then went on tour and did *Candida* another 323 times. The reaction everywhere was good, in many instances the company played to full houses and Olivia felt an understandable sense of satisfaction. In June she returned to Hollywood to

Marcus Goodrich visits his wife and son Benjamin in hospital in September 1949.

make her first picture in three years, playing opposite Richard Burton in his first American film, *My Cousin Rachel*. The Daphne Du Maurier gothic brought Olivia back to the realm of costumed movie glamor, from which she had been absent far too long, but its impact was not strong enough to really give her film career the lift that it now needed.

In retrospect it is obvious that *The Heiress* in 1949 was the high-water mark in the career of Olivia de Havilland. She would continue to be a famous and admired actress, but the peak had been passed. She had made a very deliberate decision to give at least as much time to her personal life as her professional, and she could, with a shrewdness that is characteristic, assess the facts of life as they pertained to her. "Famous people feel that they must perpetually be on the crest of the wave, not realizing that this is against all the rules of life. You can't be on top all the time, it isn't natural."

When she returned to do *Rachel* she returned minus her husband. Divorce papers were filed in August of 1952 and became final the following year, when she would meet the man who would become her second husband. In April of that year Olivia was invited by the French government to attend the Cannes Film Festival and it was there she began to be courted by Pierre Galante, one of the executive editors of the distinguished French journal *Paris Match*. Later that summer she again appeared on the stage, this time at the La Jolla (California) Playhouse in *The Dazzling Hour*. The playhouse in those years was largely supported by a group of Hollywood stars, who, lacking a showcase for their stage aspirations in Los Angeles, used this one in the delightful San Diego suburb. The event was a marked local success and Olivia turned her attentions back to Pierre Galante. Their courtship proceeded during her making of *That Lady* in Europe, but their plans to marry were complicated by the French restrictions relating to a divorced woman marrying a Catholic. It became necessary for her to reside in France for a nine-month period in order to meet government approval; she and Galante were married, on April 2, 1955, in the fishing village of Yvoy le Marron. They set up home on the right bank in Paris and Olivia became a French housewife, albeit an affluent one who would delight in Parisian society. Six years later she would publish her book, *Every Frenchman Has One*, a title which became instantly less saucy when she explained that it referred to the liver. The charming book, an account of her sometimes amusing attempts at adapting to French life, sold well and prompted reviewers to suggest another volume from a lady who obviously had some stylish ability as a writer. She replied that there would one day be an autobiography, but it has yet to appear.

Olivia gave birth to her daughter Gisele on July 18, 1956, and her life as Madame Galante appeared to be highly satisfying, especially since her husband was not adverse to her making an occasional film. These assignments required her to spend periods in Hollywood and England, although her best movie at this time was *Light in the Piazza*, made in Italy in 1961. In the early part of 1962 she proceeded to New York to appear in what would become her most successful venture in the theatre, the play *The Gift of Time* by Garson Kanin, which he had adapted from the book *Death of a Man* by Lael Tucker Wertenbaker. Olivia played Mrs. Wertenbaker in this autobiographical account of the lingering death of her husband by cancer, and Henry Fonda played the husband. The critical response was positive although the grim nature of the material precluded its popularity. Opening at the Ethel Barrymore Theatre, it ran for 90 performances and brought Olivia her best notices as a stage actress.

The success in New York came at a time when things were clearly amiss in her marriage. A year later she admitted that she and Galante had arrived at an amicable understanding; they agreed to live together in the same house but not as man and wife. This remarkable situation would go on for a dozen years or so before resolving itself in divorce. As with all the deeply personal matters of her life, Olivia has chosen never to discuss this publicly. From her earliest days in Hollywood to the present, hers has been a very private life.

During the making of Libel *in England in June 1959, Olivia is visited by her three-year-old daughter Giselle. . .*

Olivia was next seen in Hollywood when she became a presenter at the Academy Awards in April of 1963, and handed an Oscar to Sam Spiegel for his production of *Lawrence of Arabia*. Following that she went to Paramount to do the most controversial film of her career, *Lady in a Cage*, which showed her as a wealthy matron victimized and brutalized by city hoodlums. The film's overly graphic violence turned off both critics and the public, but she fared better supporting Bette Davis in *Hush . . . Hush, Sweet Charlotte* in 1965. This would be her last starring role in a major theatrical film. Five years would go by before she was seen on the screen again, in Paramount's disastrous production of *The Adventurers*, in which she performed a small role in what the trade had now come to call "star cameo parts." This would be the pattern from here on—the famous actress called upon to play short but conspicuous roles and receiving cameo billing. Her name was, and is, one with which to reckon.

Olivia had held off doing television because she disliked its dramatically dubious practice of breaking up story lines with commercials. Like many others who felt the same way, she would gradually change her

along with husband Pierre Gallante

mind and occasionally appear in the medium when offered something interesting. And like others she would realize that with the big screen offering veteran players less and less, the little screen was an increasingly important outlet. Her first major television production was *Noon Wine,* as part of the ABC *Stage 67* series, on November 23, 1966. It paired her with Jason Robards, Jr., playing a troubled Texas rancher, with Olivia as his harrassed wife, and it was directed by Sam Peckinpah, then in the early stages of a powerful but checkered career. The teleplay was well received and resulted in offers of employment from other producers, but Olivia had decided to be very economical with her appearances in TV. She was next seen on January 29, 1968, in *The Last Hunters* on NBC, a story about a British army officer (Richard Todd) trailing Nazi war criminals in the postwar years. Olivia prefers to forget this one. She would let another four years go by before agreeing to be involved in television again. By this time the television feature film had become a definite form, as well as an interesting vehicle for the appearance of famous Hollywood names, and she signed to star as *The Screaming Woman,* shown on ABC on

At home in Paris with Benjamin and Giselle, 1963

January 29, 1972. Her understanding was that this story of a woman who returns home after recovering from a nervous breakdown and tries desperately to get someone to believe that a woman has been buried alive near her house would be filmed and released under the title *The Scream.* She was so incensed when the title was changed that she tried to have her lawyer stop the change, but to no avail. She claims that she would not have done the film with "such an atrocious title. I would never do anything with that title." Producer Bill Frye later apologized to her for the title change and he also gave in to her demand that she be paid for the twelve days she worked on the picture and not the ten days contracted for. Frye found out, as have others, that Olivia is not a lady to cross. Her manners may be patrician but they are also firm, sometime almost frighteningly firm. Her anger appears the more so because it emanates from a lady, and the clarity of her diction makes it impossible not to understand what it is that provokes the anger.

Aside from appearances on talk shows and partial narration on documentaries about Hollywood, Olivia's only major television appearance in recent years has been on the greatly successful series *Roots,* in which she played a Southern lady, the wife of a man played by her old friend Henry Fonda.

She was not much in evidence on the big screen during the seventies. Her role in *Pope Joan* (1972) went mostly unnoticed, since the film failed to get bookings in America and did poorly in Europe. Five years went by and then she turned up as one of the star cameos of *Airport '77,* as a lively, wealthy art dealer, playing much the same kind of woman she is in person—outgoing, talkative, generous and humorous. After that she went to Vienna to play another cameo, as Queen Anne in the Dumas-derived *Behind the Iron Mask,* but it was another picture that quickly sank from sight. Olivia was back in Hollywood in 1978 as one of the many name players Irwin Allen used in his disaster epic, *The Swarm,* where the sight of her being stung to death by bees could hardly have pleased her faithful admirers. On the other hand it is doubtful if her old admirers go to see movies like *The Swarm.* They would more likely settle for watching her old films on television or attending retrospective showings in tribute to her, of which these have been major presentations in New York and Los Angeles. Those who attend these retrospectives can be certain that the star subject will always be elegantly gowned, glamorous and gracious, and loquacious on the topic of what an interesting and vital place Hollywood *used* to be.

When asked to talk about her success as an actress, Olivia explains that she has never had any definite technique because she never had any academic training in acting. Her approach has always been intuitive and has come from a deep study of the character she is about to play, by imagining what it would be like to be inside that character. It is a simple, intelligent, and fundamental method, and for her it has worked beauti-

At a New York retrospective showing of Warner Bros. classics in 1976, and happy recollections of an old friend

fully. "I think one can group actors into three categories: there are those performers whose attractive appearance and agreeable personality are the essential qualities, which, when well presented, bring them success. Then there are those performers whose success depends on real acting ability. Some of this group will study their own characteristics and mannerisms and develop them into a style which is appealing to the public and which comes to distinguish all their work. They tend to choose roles through which they can best express this style, something they do with a high degree of skill. The third group has a different aim and objective. Here the performer desires to divorce his own personality as much as possible from the part to be played, and to assume, instead, as completely as he can, the personality of the role itself. I found that the group to which I really wanted to belong was this group."

In 1974 Olivia received an invitation to be part of a dinner honoring

Jack L. Warner. At first surprised, she quickly realized she should accept and that it would give her a chance to show her old employer that she bore him no grudge, despite his lack of interest in her career when under his banner. He appeared delighted with her charm and he admitted, as he had on previous occasions, that she had "licked me" in their court battle of 1943 and that for the good of the industry it was probably the best thing that could have happened. The dinner marked his receiving a humanitarian award and Olivia raised a laugh by telling the gathering, "I really am all for humanitarianism and I feel it should be encouraged, especially in Jack·Warner."

In addition to the perpetual tributes to *Gone With the Wind* throughout the world, at which she is duly expected to turn up since she is one of the few survivors, Olivia has been seen in many American cities in the past decade as a lecturer. Her lecture "From the City of the Stars to the City of Light" is mostly about Hollywood and a little about Paris. In the spring of each year, and sometimes the fall as well, she tours with this program of reminiscenses and pleases her audiences with her charm and wit and her ability to tell stories. She uses no film clips, nor need she. The elocution she learned long ago from her mother (who died in 1975 at the age of eighty-seven) has matured into eloquence, happily matched with a vast recollection about the golden years of the movies.

Like all survivors of those golden years, Olivia is sad about an industry that is only a patch of what it used to be and about a Hollywood that is nowhere near what it was. What makes her most angry is the calibre of people who now govern the entertainment business in California, where she feels she could no longer live because these people are constantly offensive. In an interview with Joyce Haber for *The Los Angeles Times,* Olivia confided, "The TV business is soul-crushing, talent-destroying and human-being destroying. These men in their black towers don't know what they are doing. It's slave labor. There's no elegance left in anybody. They have no taste. Movies are being financed by conglomerates which take a write-off if they don't work. The only people who fight for what the public deserves are artists."

No one can say that Olivia de Havilland has not put up a good fight.

THE FILMS

With Dick Powell

A MIDSUMMER NIGHT'S DREAM

1935
A Warner Bros. Picture,
Produced by Jack L. Warner, with Henry Blanke,
Directed by Max Reinhardt and William Dieterle,
Script by Charles Kenyon and Mary McCall, based on Shakespeare,
Photographed by Hal Mohr,
Music by Felix Mendelssohn, arranged and conducted by Erich Wolfgang Korngold,
132 minutes.

CAST:

Bottom (James Cagney); *Lysander* (Dick Powell); *Flute* (Joe E. Brown); *Helena* (Jean Muir); *Snout* (Hugh Herbert); *Theseus* (Ian Hunter); *Quince* (Frank McHugh); *Oberon* (Victor Jory); *Hermia* (Olivia de Havilland); *Demetrius* (Ross Alexander); *Egeus* (Grant Mitchell); *Prima Ballerina Fairy* (Nina Theilade); *Hippolyta* (Verree Teasdale); *Titania* (Anita Louise); *Puck* (Mickey Rooney); *Snug* (Dewey Robinson); *Philostrate* (Hobart Cavanaugh); *Starveling* (Otis Harlan); *Ninny's Tomb* (Arthur Treacher); *Pease Blossom* (Katherine Frey); *Cobweb* (Helen Westcott); *Moth* (Fred Sale); *Mustard Seed* (Billy Barty).

No film actress has started a career in a more *de luxe* manner than Olivia de Havilland, or with greater ease. The stress and strain which usually accompanies breaking into the movies were absent for Olivia. Max Reinhardt had decided that she would be his Hermia in his prestigious film version of *A Midsummer Night's Dream* and that was that.

Reinhardt (1873–1943) was an Austrian but his fame as a stage producer of great imagination came from his years in Berlin, from 1903 to 1932. He staged the plays of Shaw, Moliere, Ibsen, and Strindberg, but Shakespeare was his first love and *A Midsummer Night's Dream* was the play with which he made an indelible impression. He thought that of all the Shakespearean plays this was the one, because of its visual imagery and fantasy factors, that could most easily be turned into a film. He loved the score Mendelssohn had written in 1843 and insisted, once he had signed his contract with Warners, that Erich Wolfgang Korngold be brought from Vienna to arrange and conduct the music. Reinhardt and Korngold had worked together with great success on several theatrical projects and they shared views about the use of music and dance in the projected screen version. Critical response was uneven about the film and it has been a debatable item over the years, but most reviewers agree that Korngold's scoring is one of the really memorable facets of the picture. Since there was not quite enough music in Mendelssohn's stage score, Korngold augmented his version with snippets from the *Italian* and the *Scotch* symphonies, and certain of the *Songs Without Words*.

That Reinhardt's epic film should be produced by Warners is still something of a mystery. The brothers Warner were noted for being tough businessmen and very frugal in their budgeting. They also specialized in everyday, realistic stories and worked up a reputation as a kind of "working class" studio. Perhaps it was because of this that Jack L. Warner laid out the astonishing (by 1934 standards) budget of a million and a half dollars on a plunge into Culture. The end result was a peculiar hybrid of a film, somehow uniting Teutonic impressionism with Hollywood casting. Warners called the shots and decided to use most of the players then under contract, even Dick Powell, their top singer, who years later admitted he never did fully understand his lines as Lysander. Powell was an Arkansan by birth and his reading of the line, "The course of true love

With Ross Alexander, Dick Powell, and Jean Muir.

never did run smooth," almost invites a "Y'all" as a tag. Those of his colleagues with some stage training, such as Ian Hunter as the king, fared better, but most of the players can be credited only with doing the best they could. James Cagney's Bottom is a pent-up coil of vitality and Mickey Rooney's leprechaun-like Puck is mischief personified. Whether they are "good Shakespeare" is still open to question.

The play, thought to have had its first performance at the Globe Theatre in London in, or around, 1595, takes place in Athens and a nearby forest. The plot concerns members of the aristocracy, a group of artisans who are putting on a play to amuse the royal court, and certain creatures of the night, or fairies. Because she refuses to marry Demetrius (Ross Alexander), the choice of her father (Grant Mitchell), Hermia (Olivia), in love with Lysander (Dick Powell), is threatened with punishment by Theseus, the Duke of Athens (Ian Hunter), who is himself about to be wed to Hippolyta, the Queen of the Amazons (Verree Teasdale).

Hermia and Lysander elope and take refuge in the nearby woods. Demetrius pursues them and is in turn pursued by Helena (Jean Muir), who is madly in love with Demetrius. At the same time the artisans pro-

With Mickey Rooney

ceed into the woods to rehearse their play in time for the Duke's wedding. Shortly thereafter the woods are visited by a group of fairies, the supernatural creatures of the night, whose rulers, Oberon (Victor Jory) and Titania (Anita Louise), are having a lover's quarrel. To avenge himself for Titania's fickle behavior, Oberon instructs the mischievous young Puck (Mickey Rooney) to drop into Titania's eyes the juice of a passion flower, which will cause her to become infatuated with the first living creature she sees upon awakening.

Puck, witnessing the artisans at their rehearsal, takes the playful notion of using the potion to turn the head of Bottom (James Cagney) into that of an ass. He further sees to it that this is the creature Titania first sees. She immediately falls madly in love with the strange-looking Bottom. Puck also uses the potion to change the affections of the four lovers, with Hermia and Lysander hating each other. But with the departure of Oberon, Titania, Puck, and all the fairies, the confusion is lifted. Bottom regains his real head, the lovers revert to the proper partners, the artisans clumsily perform their "tragical comedy" at court and raise a great deal of mirth, and the royal couple start their married life with pomp and ceremony.

With Verree Teasdale, Ian Hunter, Grant Mitchell, Dick Powell, and Ross Alexander.

A Midsummer Night's Dream was given a great amount of publicity and ballyhoo, and a lavish premiere in Hollywood, but it failed to earn its money back and found little enthusiasm with the average moviegoers. It turned out to be Max Reinhardt's only motion picture. Due to the length of time he had taken to make it and his rather soft attitude toward such things as budgets and schedules, no other Hollywood studios showed any interest in hiring the otherwise revered producer. Soon after production started it was apparent that he did not know how to manage a large and complicated film unit. Warners quickly assigned him William Dieterle, a former German actor who had worked for Reinhardt and who had begun his career as a director in Hollywood in 1930. It was understood that Reinhardt would do all the directing of the actors and that his so-called assistant would handle the direction of the camera crews and the various artisans responsible for sets and costumes. It all took much longer than anyone planned. At the outset there was little cohesion in planning the sets and allowing for photography. Massive sets had to be cut back because they could not accommodate the movements of the cameras. People were fired and hired. Warners were used to the gargantuan choreography of Busby Berkeley and not the delicate and fanciful ideas of

On location with Ross Alexander, Dick Powell, and Jean Muir.

57

Bronislava Nijinska and Nina Theilade (who also performed as the leading ballerina).

Scholars were appalled that Shakespeare's text had been cut back by as much as half but more reasonable critics realized that the producers had to think in terms of running time—over two hours anyway—and that this was a film, a visual experience. As such they agreed that Reinhardt had achieved something remarkable: He had conveyed the poetry of the original and added his own concepts about the creatures of the night, the fairies, and the fantasy. In short, it was not merely a lavish recording of the work, it was a personal translation. It is effective on its own terms and there are moments, such as fairies dancing down moonbeams and Oberon sweeping them all up in his magic cloak at dawn, that linger in the memory as incredible pieces of pure cinema. In fact, it is these dramatically visual moments that dominate Reinhardt's *A Midsummer Night's Dream* and tend to push aside the actors.

For Olivia de Havilland it was, as we have already said, a perfectly wonderful way to start a career in the movies. It resulted in the signing of a seven-year contract with Warner Bros. at a starting salary of two hundred dollars a week and quite a number of nice notices, such as the one in the *San Francisco Examiner:* "This girl is a wonder . . . when she acts Hermia she is everything."

ALIBI IKE

1935
A Warner Bros. Picture,
Produced by Edward Chodorov,
Directed by Ray Enright,
Written by William Wister, based on a story by Ring Lardner,
Photographed by Arthur Todd,
Music direction by Leo F. Forbstein,
73 minutes.

CAST:

Frank X. Farrell (Joe E. Brown); *Dolly* (Olivia de Havilland); *Cary* (Roscoe Karns); *Cap* (William Frawley); *Owner* (Joseph King); *Bess* (Ruth Donnelly); *Crawford* (Paul Harvey); *Jack Mack* (Eddie Shubert); *Lieutenant* (Pat Collins); *Minister* (Spencer Charters); *Smitty* (Gene Morgan); *Reporter* (Jack Norton).

The first film in which Olivia de Havilland was displayed to moviegoers was *Alibi Ike*, released in July of 1935, four months before *A Midsummer Night's Dream*. *The Irish in Us* was released in August. The Shakespearean extravaganza had not only taken a long time to film but a long time to assemble, and the publicity department believed it needed all the build-up of public interest it could get. For Olivia it was a bit of a rude shock to be transported from the euphoria of the Reinhardt milieu to the workaday business of a routine movie product such as *Alibi Ike*, which was simply a Joe E. Brown comedy, period. All it required was a pretty girl to play opposite him and be appealing. Olivia felt she deserved to be given more elegant material and complained to production executive Henry Blanke, who put in a word for her to that effect with Jack L. Warner. Mr. Warner's view was that she was under contract, being paid a weekly wage, and needed to be seen.

Joe E. Brown never scaled the great heights of movie stardom but maintained a firm popularity with two and three pictures a year for Warners all through the Thirties. *Alibi Ike* is a good sample of his genial idiocy, which fell somewhere between Harold Lloyd's and Stan Laurel's in style. Like Lloyd he usually got the girl and like Laurel he somehow triumphed over his own bumbling efforts to get along in a cruel world. In this outing he is a crack baseball pitcher with a major league team, who gets the nickname "Alibi" because he has elaborate excuses for whatever errors he makes and is forever apologizing about his gauche behavior. Missing a pitch, for example, he says, "I don't bat my best on Wednesdays." He is, however, a first-rate pitcher with an eccentric style

and among his many admirers is Dolly (Olivia), the sister of the wife (Ruth Donnelly) of the team's owner (Joseph King). Smitten with the lovely young girl, one day he shoves an engagement ring on her finger. She accepts him but later breaks off the engagement when he makes some flippant remarks to which she takes exception. Alibi is kidnapped by racketeers who need to deprive his team of his skill so that their bets on the other team will pay off. But he escapes and after a wild chase manages to get back to the field in time to save the game. This, of course, also brings Dolly back into his arms.

Overlooking the fact that a refined eighteen-year-old was hardly likely to be attracted to a roughneck baseball player in his mid-forties, *Alibi Ike* is a mildly amusing little comedy. Olivia may have felt somewhat demoted in having to do it but she was at least learning something about the picture business. Those who worked with her also learned something about her. They quickly found she was not the average starlet. Sensing that she had come off the Shakespearean picture with a rather cultured, grand manner, the crew of *Alibi Ike* dunked her in a pond to teach her a lesson in humility. Shortly afterwards, while filming the scene in which Alibi Ike clumsily tips a canoe while trying to court her on the pond, Olivia went over the side, took a deep breath and held her nose under water for as long as she could stay down. It caused consternation among the crew, who thought perhaps she had drowned. They learned that this was a young lady with not only a good sense of humor but a lot of determination.

With Joe E. Brown

THE IRISH IN US

1935
A Warner Bros. First National Picture,
Produced by Samuel Bischoff,
Directed by Lloyd Bacon,
Written by Earl Baldwin, based on a story by Frank Orsatti,
Photographed by George Barnes,
Music direction by Leo F. Forbstein,
Running time: 84 minutes.

CAST:

Danny O'Hara (James Cagney); *Pat O'Hara* (Pat O'Brien); *Lucille Jackson* (Olivia de Havilland); *Mike O'Hara* (Frank McHugh); *Car-Barn* (Allen Jenkins); *Ma O'Hara* (Mary Gordon); *Captain Jackson* (J. Farrell MacDonald); *Doc Mullins* (Thomas Jackson); *Joe Delaney* (Harvey Perry).

The Irish strain in American culture found much outlet during the Golden Age of Hollywood and the studio where it reared its head most enthusiastically was Warners. The qualities of Irish humor and charm laced many a Warner picture and more often than not those pictures featured the likes of James Cagney, Pat O'Brien, Frank McHugh, and a full phalanx of Celtic character actors. It was in this emerald environment that Olivia de Havilland somewhat bewilderingly found herself for her next assignment. She may have believed that it was not her scene but it was already beginning to dawn on her that the main function of a fledgling contract player was to turn up for work, where and when told.

The title, *The Irish in Us*, told the customers what to expect— a knockabout comedy spiced with blarney. The story is that of three brothers, living with their widowed mother (Mary Gordon) in New York. Danny (Cagney) is a scamp who doesn't much care for ordinary lines of work and looks to make money as a fight promoter, to the disgust of serious, sober Pat (O'Brien), a policeman. The other brother, Mike (McHugh), is a city fireman and none too bright. Pat falls in love with Lucille (de Havilland), the daughter of his superior officer (J. Farrell MacDonald) and brings her home to meet mother and the boys. Danny takes an immediate shine to the lovely young lady and woos her away from Pat with very little effort. A frost sets in between the two brothers.

Inspired to improve his monetary standing, Danny picks up and signs a dim-witted fighter named Car-Barn Hammerschlog (Allen Jenkins) and matches him with a champion (Harvey Perry). Unfortunately Mike decides to celebrate with Car-Barn before the fight and the two become stupifyingly drunk. Rather than call off the fight and lose money, Danny steps into the ring and takes over Car-Barn's role. And wins. By this time Pat realizes he has lost Lucille and that he has lost her to a brother who is really quite a guy. A kiss on the cheek from Lucille helps soften the loss.

The Irish in Us is nothing more than a routine Cagney movie of its time, and one which he himself refers to merely as "product." It received the fast-paced, head-on-humor it needed, thanks to director Lloyd Bacon, who had long had a reputation as a fast and very capable workman. Indeed, this was but one of five films he directed in 1935, three of them with Cagney. For Olivia the film offered nothing other than exposure to the public as a sweet and pretty young newcomer. But she could take heart from the comments of the review in *Variety:* "She gives every indication of a gal who can be steered into lights. Class looking, she also has a warm personality and seems to know what it's all about, even in the midst of boxing gloves and ad-lib slapstick." Marking time in a couple of programmers may not have pleased Olivia at the time but they served the purpose. Her lot was about to improve considerably.

With James Cagney and Allen Jenkins

With Pat O'Brien and James Cagney

With Frank McHugh, Mary
Gordon, James Cagney, and
Pat O'Brien

CAPTAIN BLOOD

1935
A Warner Bros. First National Picture,
A Cosmopolitan Production,
Produced by Hal B. Wallis,
Directed by Michael Curtiz,
Written by Casey Robinson, based on the novel by Rafael Sabatini,
Photographed by Hal Mohr,
Music by Erich Wolfgang Korngold,
119 minutes.

CAST:

Peter Blood (Errol Flynn); *Arabella Bishop* (Olivia de Havilland); *Colonel Bishop* (Lionel Atwill); *Captain Levasseur* (Basil Rathbone); *Jeremy Pitt* (Ross Alexander); *Hagthorpe* (Guy Kibbee); *Lord Willoughby* (Henry Stephenson); *Wolverstone* (Robert Barrat); *Dr. Bronson* (Hobart Cavanaugh); *Dr. Whacker* (Donald Meek); *Mrs. Barlowe* (Jessie Ralph); *Honesty Nuttall* (Forrester Harvey); *Reverend Ogle* (Frank McGlynn, Sr.); *Captain Gardner* (Holmes Herbert); *Andrew Baynes* (David Torrence); *Cahusac* (J. Carrol Naish); *Don Diego* (Pedro de Cordoba); *Governor Steed* (George Hassell); *Kent* (Harry Cording); *Baron Jeffreys* (Leonard Mudie).

As every film buff knows, *Captain Blood* is the film that made an immediate star of Errol Flynn and triggered one of the most colorful careers in movie history. But it also made a star of Olivia de Havilland. Despite having had star roles in three pictures, her impact had not been great. With the success of *Captain Blood* and the potent qualities resulting from the teaming with Flynn, her own career was now firmly set. Her role as Arabella Bishop was also the most interesting she had been given in her first year in the business. It is often thought that Olivia's Flynn assignments relegated her to little more than decoration. This is not true of Arabella Bishop—or of Maid Marian or Elizabeth Bacon Custer. Arabella is good humored and enterprising. She is in fact entirely responsible for Peter Blood's salvation.

Because of his success as *The Count of Monte Cristo* (1934), Robert Donat was sought by Warners to play Peter Blood. The British actor at first agreed, but he was an asthmatic and later decided that the strenuous role would likely be too much for him. Had Donat played Blood his co-star would have been Jean Muir, but once Flynn was given the role it occurred to the studio to match him with Olivia. It was one of those decisions around which careers and fortunes sometimes turn. The fact that Olivia and Flynn had a genuine attraction to each other was, of course, a salient factor. Additionally they were perfection for a story of historical romance, what with their classic good looks, cultured speaking voices, and a sense of distant aristocracy about them.

Flynn arrived at the Burbank Studios of Warner Bros. in January of 1935, having been brought from London and signed on the basis of his work as the lead in a B picture, *Murder at Monte Carlo*. He did little during the first half of the year other than a bit in *The Case of the Curious Bride* and a small part in *Don't Bet on Blondes*. It was during this period that he courted Lili Damita, then working at Warners with James Cagney in *Frisco Kid*, and married her in June. Flynn never gave Damita much credit for his luck but the fact that she was an old friend of director Michael Curtiz and also socialized with the wives of Jack and Harry Warner must surely have had something to do with his being considered for *Blood*.

The film, which was a re-make of the 1923 version starring J. Warren Kerrigan, also did much to further the career of Curtiz. He joined Warners in 1926 after a dozen years making pictures in his native

With George Hassell, Mary Forbes, and Lionel Atwill

Hungary and in Germany, but although he was a respected and reliable director prior to *Blood,* it was afterwards that his prestige truly blossomed. He revealed a flair for action sequences and swift pacing that was to come to prominence in several other Flynn swashbucklers, as well as a variety of dramas, musicals, and comedies. Curtiz was *the* Warner Bros. director and the careers of Flynn and Olivia de Havilland would have been much different without the association of this forceful, dynamic, imaginative, and often harsh taskmaster.

The year is 1685, a time of rebellion in England. The attempts to unseat the brutal James II fail and those rebels who are not hanged are sent as slaves to the sulphur mines and plantations of Jamaica. Among them is Peter Blood, an Irish doctor arrested and tried for giving aid to a wounded rebel officer. On the dock at Port Royal he and the others are sold as laborers. Blood is impertinent to the island's most prominent plantation owner, Colonel Bishop (Lionel Atwill), who passes him up. When it seems Blood will be bought by a much crueler master, the colonel's niece Arabella bids for Blood and wins him. She tells him that he is fortunate that she was on hand and he bitterly replies, "I hardly consider

With Harry Cording and Errol Flynn

it fortunate to be bought by anyone with the name of Bishop." Surprised at his ingratitude she tells him, "You are hardly in a position to have anything to say about it."

Blood's lot as a slave soon improves when he is appointed physician to the gout-ridden governor (George Hassell), an appointment brought about by Arabella. Again he finds it hard to be grateful. Taking advantage of his freedom to move around the island, Blood plans an escape for himself and his friends, and discusses the purchase of a boat. Arabella spots him doing this but keeps it to herself. Later she speaks up at the plantation when Blood cannot account for his movements. She tells her uncle that Blood was with her. At their next meeting he finally expresses gratitude, but oversteps the mark and gets his face slapped.

Spaniards attack and sack Port Royal, and Blood takes over their galleon and puts to sea as a privateer. His fame as a pirate builds until his name is dreaded, so much so that a French rival, Levasseur (Basil Rathbone) coaxes Blood into a partnership so they may dominate the sea lanes together. In the meantime Bishop is appointed governor of Jamaica and Arabella visits relatives in England. On her return voyage her ship is attacked by Levasseur and she is captured, along with Lord Willoughby (Henry Stephenson), who has a commission for Blood as captain of the Royal Navy. James II has fled to France after being replaced by William III, and England is at war with the French.

Filming the slave auction. Director Michael Curtiz, wearing a T-shirt, is left of camera.

With Errol Flynn

With Henry Stephenson and Errol Flynn

On the island of Virgen Magra, Levasseur decides he wants Arabella for himself, but the arrival of Blood provokes bad feelings with the amorous Frenchman. He points out that personal spoils must be divided as specified in their signed articles. Levasseur is offended when Blood meets the price set upon Arabella and flings pearls to the French crew. The two captains draw swords and Levasseur loses his life. Arabella is not pleased and tells Blood, "I don't wish to be bought by you." He takes satisfaction in replying, "As a lady once said to a slave—you are hardly in a position to have anything to say about it."

On the voyage to Jamaica Arabella tells Blood she despises him for the way he has lived as a pirate, but Lord Willoughby rightly senses she really loves him. His Lordship breaks the news of the turn of events in England and Blood accepts his commission. Arriving at Port Royal they find it under attack by two French warships. Blood engages them in combat; one of the warships is soon destroyed when its powder magazines receive a direct hit, and the other is boarded and captured. Colonel Bishop returns to Port Royal and is stripped of his post as governor for leaving it in time of war to engage in his personal hunt for Blood. Lord Willoughby advises him that his fortunes now rest with the new governor. Entering the office Bishop is astounded to find that the new governor is Peter Blood, who, with Arabella by his side, cheerfully says, "Good morning, Uncle."

Captain Blood was released in December of 1935 and won good notices

and wide public approval at once. It was clearly a winner. The film started a new era for costumed adventure epic, with more style and flair than they had ever received before. It was also the first music score written by Erich Wolfgang Korngold for the screen and paved the way for great improvements in film composition. Flynn and Curtiz went on to greater glory and Olivia de Havilland could take pride and satisfaction in her contribution. Arabella Bishop is no mere cardboard heroine. She is a feisty beauty, whose pretty head contains clear notions of what she wants. Fortunately for Peter Blood, she wanted him.

ANTHONY ADVERSE

1936
A Warner Bros. Picture,
Produced by Henry Blanke,
Directed by Mervyn LeRoy,
Written by Sheridan Gibney, based on the novel by Hervey Allen,
Photographed by Tony Gaudio,
Music by Erich Wolfgang Korngold,
139 minutes.

CAST:

Anthony Adverse (Fredric March); *Angela Guisseppe* (Olivia de Havilland); *Maria* (Anita Louise); *John Bonnyfeather* (Edmund Gwenn); *Don Luis* (Claude Rains); *Vincente Nolte* (Donald Woods); *Dennis Moore* (Louis Hayward); *Faith* (Gale Sondergaard); *Carlo Cibo* (Akim Tamiroff); *Neleta* (Steffi Duna); *Anthony at ten* (Billy Mauch); *Father Xavier* (Henry O'Neill); *De Bruille* (Ralph Morgan); *Ouvrard* (Fritz Leiber); *Tony Guisseppe* (Luis Alberni); *Angela as a child* (Ann Howard); *Napoleon Bonaparte* (Rollo Lloyd); *Sancho* (George E. Stone); *Captain Jorham* (Joseph Crehan); *Mrs. Jorham* (Clara Blandick); *Anthony as a little boy* (Scotty Beckett).

Hervey Allen's epic novel of historical romance, *Anthony Adverse*, was published in 1933 and quickly became a best seller, even to the extent of being translated into more than a dozen languages. It was inevitable that it would find its way to the screen, but in selling it to Warner Bros. the author expressed concern about the likely treatment. He need not have worried about the excellent production values Warners would give the film, including a truly sumptuous score by Erich Korngold, but even with a running time of almost two hours and twenty minutes, there was no way to really accommodate Allen's lengthy story. Nowadays *Anthony Adverse* would probably be done as a television mini-series. In 1936 it was decided to give the title role to the handsome and popular Fredric March, although at thirty-nine he was a little too old for the part. The casting of Olivia de Havilland as Angela, the young girl he loves, was an excellent choice and a solid step forward for her after the success of *Captain Blood*.

The title character gets his name because he is a son of adversity. He is the illegitimate result of a passion between a young army officer (Louis Hayward) and Maria (Anita Louise), the young wife of a Spanish grandee, Don Luis (Claude Rains). The officer loses his life in a duel with Don Luis and the infant is deposited on the steps of a convent, where he is

With Edmund Gwenn, Fredric March, Gale Sondergaard, Clara Blandick, and Joseph Crehan

brought up and educated by Father Xavier (Henry O'Neill). At the age of ten Anthony is taken to the home of a Scottish merchant, John Bonnyfeather (Edmund Gwenn), in the city of Leghorn, where he grows up to become an apprentice to Bonnyfeather. For some strange reason the Scotsman feels a spiritual bond with the boy. Bonnyfeather is, in fact, his grandfather, although he does not know it.

Anthony finds happiness in the Bonnyfeather home, particularly growing up with Angela, the daughter of the cook (Luis Alberni). When they mature they become lovers and resolve to spend their lives together. Angela has a fine singing voice and during a cart ride through the woods with Anthony she sings to him:

Though the spring will not linger forever,
And this day will return to us never,
Though each vow we made,
In your memory fade,
I'll wait still for you, my love,
I'll wait for you, my love.

Olivia is the center girl in the first of the film's opera sequences.

The song (with lyrics by Howard Koch, set to a beguiling Korngold melody, and voice dubbed by Diana Gaylen) is a perfect expression of young love. At this stage in their lives it seems that nothing could be better for Anthony and Angela.

Their idyll is shattered when the cook comes into some money and takes his family away from Leghorn. Anthony is thereafter assigned by Bonnyfeather to travel and oversee his business interests in various places. During the course of these travels he attends an opera and finds Angela to be one of the chorus. They delight in resuming their lives together and marry (a concession to film censorship) but they lose track of each other when Angela has to leave for a job and the note she places for Anthony is blown away.

Years pass and Anthony becomes hardened by his experiences, particularly when he is assigned to Cuba and almost succumbs to boredom and drink. Returning to Leghorn he finds Bonnyfeather has died and that his assistant Faith (Gale Sondergaard) has formed an alliance with Don Luis to cheat him out of his inheritance from Bonnyfeather. They are eventually defeated in their plans. Anthony prospers in business and travels to

Paris. It is there that he again sees Angela, who is now an acclaimed opera star and, unknown to Anthony, the mistress of Napoleon Bonaparte (Rollo Lloyd). Angela is also a mother and Anthony is enchanted to find he has a son. However, his resolve to pick up his life with Angela is doomed. Her fame and her position as Napoleon's mistress cannot be kept from him and the lovers decide they must part. Angela sadly decides to give Anthony custody of their son, and sends them to start a new life in America.

Anthony Adverse fell short of the success Warners believed they could achieve but over the years it has maintained a certain position as a typical "golden era" epic, albeit a rather lumbering one. It was good exposure for Olivia de Havilland. She is particularly good in the first half of her role, as the sweet young Angela, uncomplicated and cheerful and totally loving. Watching her in these scenes it is easy to understand the praise given her by co-star Claude Rains, "She is a shining, glowing optimist." Olivia is, however, less effective in her later scenes as the opera star and mistress of Napoleon. She was, after all, a mere twenty and not yet enough of an actress to overcome the radiant innocence in her eyes. The courtesan of an emperor, a position fraught with intrigue, would have to be a shrewd lady. It is much more pleasurable to think of Angela as the girl sitting alongside Anthony in the cart, singing as they drive down the lane.

Filming the lane sequence. Director Mervyn LeRoy stands in front of the camera unit.

On the Fort Chukoti location at Agoura, California—west of the San Fernando Valley

With Fredric March and
Scotty Beckett

THE CHARGE OF THE LIGHT BRIGADE

1936
A Warner Bros. Picture,
Produced by Hal B. Wallis,
Directed by Michael Curtiz,
Written by Michael Jacoby and Rowland Leigh,
Photographed by Sol Polito,
Music by Max Steiner,
115 minutes.

CAST:

Major Geoffrey Vickers (Errol Flynn); *Elsa Campbell* (Olivia de Havilland); *Capt. Perry Vickers* (Patric Knowles); *Sir Charles Macefield* (Henry Stephenson); *Sir Benjamin Warrenton* (Nigel Bruce); *Colonel Campbell* (Donald Crisp); *Capt. Randall* (David Niven); *Surat Khan* (C. Henry Gordon); *Major Jowett* (George P. Huntley, Jr.); *Count Igor Volonoff* (Robert Barrat); *Lady Octavia Warrenton* (Spring Byington); *Sir Humphrey Harcourt* (E. E. Clive); *Puran Singh* (J. Carrol Naish); *Cornet Barclay* (Walter Holbrook); *Cornet Pearson* (Charles Sedgwick); *Prema Singh* (Scotty Beckett); *Colonel Woodward* (Lumsden Hare); *Prema's Mother* (Princess Baigum); *Wazir* (George Regas); *Major Anderson* (Colin Kenny); *Colonel Coventry* (Gordon Hart).

Viewed as a history lesson *The Charge of the Light Brigade* is absurd. It takes as its climax one of the most hideous blunders in British military history and precedes it with a fictional story—indeed the bulk of the film—about the British regime in India in the mid-nineteenth century. The climax is the charge made by the four regiments of light cavalry (a brigade) at Balaclava, during the Crimean War (1853–56), which England and France waged to prevent the Russians from occupying Turkey and gaining access to the Mediterranean. Despite its success, the war was dirty, brutal, and badly managed, and the charge celebrated by Tennyson in his epic poem was its most horrible folly. It achieved nothing, and five hundred of the seven hundred cavalrymen involved lost their lives. Aside from the heavy human cost, nothing about the Crimean War can be learned from watching the 1936 Warner Bros. adventure yarn.

However, if it is regarded purely as entertainment, the film is a classic. Due to his enormous impact as *Captain Blood,* Errol Flynn was swiftly geared into super stardom as the brave, dashing officer responsible for sending the Light Brigade into action. Anita Louise was cast as Elsa Campbell, his betrothed, but by the time it came to shoot her scenes she was busy in another film. With the returns on *Blood* rolling into the studio, it then seemed even better to give the part to Olivia de Havilland. Actually, Anita Louise, a regal but rather static beauty, could have played the limited role perfectly. Elsa Campbell is not nearly as interesting or as enterprising a lady as Arabella Bishop. It is largely a decorative role and during the prolonged shooting of the masculine production Olivia often became bored, especially on location. She liked to go riding but they did not want her to run the risk of injury. During the filming of an action sequence—the escape from the siege of Fort Chukoti—Flynn accidentally knocked her out with a swing of his arm. When she came to in his arms, he asked her how she felt and she replied, "Disgusted."

The invented story concerns a cavalry regiment, the 27th Lancers, stationed in northwest India in 1850. A powerful chieftain, Surat Khan (C. Henry Gordon), ambitious to evict the British and become the ruler of

With Spring Byington and Patric Knowles

82

that part of India, forms an alliance with Russia. Major Geoffrey Vickers (Flynn) is an acquaintance of the cultured Khan and during a tiger hunt saves his life. Vickers is thereafter sent to Arabia to purchase horses for the British army, in preparation for the predictable conflict building up in the Balkans. En route he stops off in Calcutta to see his commanding officer, Colonel Campbell (Donald Crisp), and daughter Elsa. He and Elsa are engaged but Elsa loves Geoffrey's brother Perry (Patric Knowles), who is a captain in army intelligence. When Perry finally summons up the courage to tell his brother of his love for Elsa, Geoffrey is at first angry and then understanding when he assumes it to be an infatuation. For her part, Elsa finds it very hard to tell Geoffrey that she loves his brother. When she finally tries, her attempts are interrupted by the attack of Surat Khan and his forces on Chukoti.

After a prolonged defense, the survivors at Chukoti surrender when the Khan offers them safe passage out of the fort and to the boats on the nearby river. Once they are at the river the survivors are gunned down, with only Vickers and Elsa allowed to get away. Surat Khan now marks

With Errol Flynn

his debt to Vickers paid. But Vickers vows vengeance on the treacherous chieftain. With the outbreak of war in the Crimea, the 27th Lancers are assigned to the British forces and Vickers finds out that the Khan is with the Russians as a guest-observer. The Light Brigade is ordered to pull back because of the vast number of Russian soldiers and artillery on the Balaclava Heights but Vickers writes a completely different order, which commands the Light Brigade to attack the heights. He forges the name of the British commander, Sir Charles Macefield (Henry Stephenson), to the order and then writes Sir Charles a letter explaining what he has done. Vickers next sends his brother away from the scene of battle to deliver a dispatch elsewhere and thereby saves him for Elsa. He addresses the men of the 27th Lancers on the field and tells them that Surat Khan is present. Then—forward the Light Brigade! By the time they reach the Russian artillery position most of the British cavalrymen have been shot from their horses but Vickers finds the Khan and the two men kill each other, Vickers by a pistol shot and the Khan with a lance through his heart. Later Sir Charles Macefield burns the letter, shields Vickers, and allows the charge to go down in history an epic of gallantry.

In 1968 Tony Richardson produced a British version of *The Charge of the Light Brigade* and told the truth about the military rivalry and stupidity which produced the wasteful charge. That version did not do well at the

Escaping the Chukoti massacre—with Flynn, of course

box office. It had a sour tone and also fell short as entertainment. The 1936 Warner Bros. is history through rose-colored glasses but it remains stirring entertainment. As for the actual charge, it is doubtful if anything like it will ever be seen again on the screen. It is a magnificently filmed action sequence, photographed and edited with the utmost skill, building and building in momentum as the hundreds of handsomely uniformed soldiers thunder down the valley amid the volleys of Russian cannonades. In filming this sequence Michael Curtiz was assisted by B. Reeves Eason, an expert second-unit director who had specialized in training and filming horses. Sadly, in order to achieve this visually splendid sequence, a number of horses were killed and many of the stuntmen injured. Due to pressure brought to bear by the Society for the Prevention of Cruelty to Animals, Hollywood was thereafter closely supervised in its treatment of horses on the screen.

Flynn claimed that this was the most difficult picture he ever made and it is easy to see why. It was not a difficult picture for Olivia, other than the stretches of location boredom, and appearing in it did her no harm. It was good to star in a box office winner but she would have to wait until her next Flynn film to get a role that would make the teaming meaningful and satisfying.

With Errol Flynn

Make-up break

*With Flynn and director
Michael Curtiz (sitting)*

With Errol Flynn

CALL IT A DAY

1937
A Warner Bros. Cosmopolitan Picture,
Produced by Hal B. Wallis,
Directed by Archie Mayo,
Written by Casey Robinson, based on the play by Dodie Smith,
Photographed by Ernest Haller,
Music direction by Loe F. Forbstein,
89 minutes.

CAST:

Catherine Hilton (Olivia de Havilland); *Roger Hilton* (Ian Hunter); *Dorothy Hilton* (Frieda Inescourt); *Joan Collette* (Anita Louise); *Muriel Weston* (Alice Brady); *Frank Haines* (Roland Young); *Ann Hilton* (Bonita Granville); *Beatrice Gwynne* (Marcia Ralston); *Ethel* (Peggy Wood); *Paul* (Walter Woolf King); *Martin Hilton* (Peter Willes); *Charwoman* (Una O'Connor); *Cook* (Beryl Mercer); *Vera* (Elsa Buchanan); *Elsie Lester* (Mary Field); *Butler* (Robert Adair).

With Peter Willes and Bonita Granville

Call It a Day is notable in the Olivia de Havilland catalogue as being the first film in which she received top billing. Aside from that, it is not a very notable picture. The Dodie Smith play on which it is based had been a success with the Theatre Guild in New York the previous year and there had been several productions elsewhere, including Los Angeles, where Joan Fontaine played the role which went to her sister in the film version. But, as is often the case, what is charming and amusing on the stage is less so under the magnifying glass of the cinema.

The story takes place in the course of a single day and involves a supposedly middle-class English family as they are smitten with spring fever. Despite the casting of several British actors, this is a very Hollywoodian version of England. Theirs is a life of absolute ease and money appears to be no problem. Catherine Hilton (Olivia) is in the process of having her portrait painted and finds herself falling in love with the handsome artist (Walter Woolf King), which does not please his wife (Peggy Wood). Catherine's father (Ian Hunter) receives the amorous attentions of an actress (Marcia Ralston), while her mother (Frieda Inescourt) does her best to ward off an old friend (Roland Young). At the same time, brother Martin (Peter Willes) goes mad about a lovely neighbor (Anita Louise) and kid sister Ann (Bonita Granville) bothers everyone with her constant gab.

With Walter Woolf King

By the end of this particular spring day, the romantic fever ebbs away

With director Archie Mayo and Walter Woolf King

and the characters come to their senses. But none too convincingly. Perhaps the strictures of 1937 film censorship took some of the tang away from Miss Smith's play. For Olivia it was a chance to romp through lightly comedic material, possibly a relief after playing a string of historical heroines, but as written and directed her role is paper thin. However, *Call It a Day* is not a film to discuss seriously. Call it a frou-frou.

With Bonita Granville

With Frieda Inescort.

THE GREAT GARRICK

1937
A Warner Bros. Picture,
Produced by Mervyn LeRoy,
Directed by James Whale,
Written by Ernst Vajda,
Photographed by Ernest Haller,
Music by Adolph Deutsch,
95 minutes.

CAST:

David Garrick (Brian Aherne); *Germaine De Le Corbe* (Olivia de Havilland); *Tubby* (Edward Everett Horton); *M. Picard* (Melville Cooper); *Basset* (Luis Alberni); *Beaumarchais* (Lionel Atwill); *Nicolle* (Marie Wilson); *Auber* (Lana Turner); *Molle* (Linda Perry); *Janin* (Craig Edwards); *Madame Moreau* (Dorothy Tree); *Moreau* (Chester Clute); *Jean Cabot* (Etienne Girardot); *Le Brun* (Albert Dekker); *Captain Thierre* (Milton Owen); *Blacksmith* (Trevor Barette); *Vendor* (E. E. Clive); *Innkeeper (Turk's Head)* (Harey Davenport); *Innkeeper (Adam and Eve)* (Paul Everton).

It is almost a rule of thumb in Hollywood that movies about the theatre do not do well. *The Great Garrick* is no exception, although it deserved more attention than it received. And still does. It was skillfully written by Ernst Vajda (based on his own play *Ladies and Gentlemen*) and stylishly directed by James Whale, with some of the darkly romantic-macabre touches that marked his *The Old Dark House* (1932) and *The Bride of Frankenstein* (1935). *The Great Garrick* is high comedy, with due credit going to Brian Aherne for his dapper performance as the celebrated English actor. Garrick (1717–1779) excelled in Shakespeare. He was a fixture of the Drury Lane Theatre, he organized the Stratford-on-Avon revivals of the great Shakespearean plays, and when he died he was buried in Westminster Abbey at the foot of Shakespeare's statue. Whether he was as handsome and dashing as Aherne is in this film is open to question.

The film makes no claim to accuracy. Indeed, Vajda tells his audience that this is purely a tale that "might have happened." It opens at the Drury Lane Theatre as Garrick concludes a performance of *Hamlet*, after which the French playwright Beaumarchais (Lionel Atwill) invites him to appear at the Comedie Francaise in Paris as the star of his new play *The Count of Seville*. He accepts but a rumor then arises that he is doing so in order to give the famed French company a lesson in the art of acting. The members of the Comedie Francaise hear about this and take great excep-

With Brian Aherne

tion to his presumed arrogance. They take over an inn on the road to Paris—The Adam and Eve Inn—and assume the functions of the staff. The French actors play the roles of loud, quarrelsome, incompetent waiters, clerks, chamber maids, and kitchen help, and make Garrick's stay at the inn thoroughly miserable. However, their attempts to make him disgusted with French manners and leave France are overplayed and he soon spots them for the actors they are. He decides not to be impressed with anything they do.

One evening a lovely young aristocrat, Germaine Dupont, the Countess de la Corbe (Olivia) arrives at the inn in a state of exhaustion, after her carriage breaks down. Germaine is in flight from her father, who wants her to marry a man she dosen't love. Garrick assumes she is a member of the Comedie Francaise and treats her romantically in order to win her heart and then abandon her. Garrick then foils the group by beating up the blacksmith who has been assigned to thrash him. He throws him in a pond, takes his clothes, blackens his face and enters the inn in the guise of the blacksmith, telling the others that he has beaten Garrick to death with his hammer. The actors of the Comedie Francaise are appalled. They swear each other to secrecy and plan to leave for Paris. Garrick then

With Melville Cooper and Brian Aherne

reveals himself and upbraids them for overplaying their parts. They beg his forgiveness and invite him to appear with their company in Paris. He accepts and leaves, but not before turning on poor Germaine and denouncing her as an inferior actress who should give up the theatre.

In Paris, Garrick realizes he has been harsh in brushing off Germaine and that he misses her. He is dismayed to find that she is not a member of the troupe and that the others think she almost spoiled their little "play" at the inn. Garrick agrees to perform *Don Juan* for the Comedie Francaise but on opening night he feels so heartsick about Germaine that he cannot play the role. He starts to make an announcement to the audience to excuse himself when he looks up at a box and spots the pretty little countess. He then speaks of his love for La Belle France. Germaine understands and throws him a rose. Cries Garrick, "Ring up the curtain. I shall play Don Juan as he was never played before."

Germaine was well within the range of the twenty-one-year-old Olivia. She fitted the part as perfectly as the gorgeous gowns she wore, playing with humor and spirit, and keeping up with an impressive group of seasoned character actors, such as Edward Everett Horton, Melville Cooper, and Luis Alberni, who was superb as the mock-chef, smashing every

With Brian Aherne

piece of crockery within range. The choice of Aherne as Garrick was also superb. He and Olivia dated during the making of the picture, probably with Warner Bros. encouragement. Two years later Aherne became her brother-in-law when he married Joan Fontaine.

*With director James Whale
and Brian Aherne*

IT'S LOVE I'M AFTER

1937
A Warner Bros. First National Picture,
Produced by Hal B. Wallis,
Directed by Archie Mayo,
Written by Casey Robinson, based on a story by Maurice Hanline,
Photographed by James Van Trees,
Music by Heinz Roemheld,
90 minutes.

CAST:

Basil Underwood (Leslie Howard); *Joyce Arden* (Bette Davis); *Marcia West* (Olivia de Havilland); *Digges* (Eric Blore); *Henry Grant* (Patric Knowles); *William West* (George Barbier); *Aunt Ella* (Spring Byington); *Gracie Kane* (Bonita Granville); *Butler* (E. E. Clive); *Elsie* (Veda Ann Borg); *Joyce's Maid* (Valerie Bergere); *Mrs. Kane* (Georgia Caine); *Mrs. Hinkle* (Sarah Edwards); *Mrs. Babson* (Grace Field); *Mr. Babson* (Harvey Clark); *Mr. Hinkle* (Thomas Pogue); *Mr. Kane* (Ed Mortimer).

With Eric Blore and Leslie Howard

Hollywood's so-called screwball comedies of the Thirties often dealt with the well-to-do and presented them as pleasant, hedonistic, and daft, especially in the area of the heart. *It's Love I'm After* is almost the perfect example. In addition, it pokes fun at "theatre folk," making them appear almost as dizzy and impractical as the wealthy set. That neither actors nor the rich could be this light-headed is of no importance. And after appearing together in two heavy dramas–*Of Human Bondage* (1934) and *The Petrified Forest* (1936)—Leslie Howard and Bette Davis probably jumped at the chance to romp through some nonsense. For Olivia de Havilland it meant third billing but it was a focal role and allowed for another fling as an amorous young socialite. Her work in *Call It a Day* seems almost like training for this one.

Basil Underwood (Howard) is a John Barrymore-like matinee idol. His co-star, Joyce Arden (Davis), is also his bride-to-be. Off-stage they are constantly battling, mostly because Basil enjoys the adulation of young ladies and is forever postponing the wedding. One such young lady is Marcia West (Olivia), who sits and drools at his every performance. One evening she comes backstage and admits she is madly in love with him. Her fiance, Henry Grant (Patric Knowles) pays his own visit to the actor and pleads for him to rebuff Marcia's attentions, since they are harming his own chances. Basil picks up the challenge of playing the role of a cad and with his long-suffering but devoted valet (Eric Blore) he descends on

With George Barbier, Eric Blore, Patric Knowles, and Spring Byington

the West mansion in Pasadena and announces himself as their guest.

With Patric Knowles

Basil behaves abominably. Marcia is thrilled with his presence and takes it as evidence of his interest in her, which causes him to act even more outrageously. Her father (George Barbier) is appalled at the antics of this arrogant invader, as are the relatives and the servants. No matter how badly Basil behaves, Marcia forgives. She construes his crude candor as honesty and excuses his manners, "What are manners? Little rules for little people!" He insults everyone, complains about everything, and disrupts the household. By now even Basil himself is beginning to worry about Marcia. He decides to force himself upon her one night in her room and frighten her with rough and ungentlemanly advances. Marcia is delighted and the next morning she announces the breaking of her engagement to Henry. In desperation Basil pleads with Joyce to come to his aid and pose as his wife. She does but not without having a little fun at Basil's expense. She encourages Marcia in her infatuation and tell's Henry he has been double-crossed. Only when Marcia declares her plans to marry Basil does Joyce make the final moves. She shows photos of two children to Marcia and claims them as her own by Basil and that this will be a case of desertion. Marcia is ashamed and, after expressing her disgust to the actor, resumes her engagement to Henry. Basil and Joyce also resume their relationship—devoted to each other personally and professionally but still bickering, even during the course of stage performances.

With Georgia Caine, Bonita Granville, and Leslie Howard

With Leslie Howard and
Bette Davis.

GOLD IS WHERE YOU FIND IT

1938
A Warner Bros. Cosmopolitan Picture,
Produced by Hal B. Wallis,
Directed by Michael Curtiz,
Written by Warren Duff and Robert Buckner, based on the novel by
   Clements Ripley,
Photographed in Technicolor by Sol Polito,
Music by Max Steiner,
91 minutes.

CAST:

Jared Whitney (George Brent); *Serena Ferris* (Olivia de Havilland); *Colonel Ferris* (Claude Rains); *Rosanne Ferris* (Margaret Lindsay); *Ralph Ferris* (John Litel); *Lanceford Ferris* (Tim Holt); *Slag Minton* (Barton MacLane); *Judge* (Henry O'Neill); *Molly Featherstone* (Marcia Ralston); *Enoch Howitt* (George F. Hayes); *Harrison McCoy* (Sidney Toler); *Crouch* (Robert McWade); *Senator Walsh* (Clarence Kolb); *McKenzie* (Russell Simpson); *Dr. Parsons* (Harry Davenport); *Joshua* (Willie Best); *Senator Hearst* (Moroni Olsen); *Nixon* (Granville Bates); *Turner* (Charles Halton); *Cryder* (Erville Alderson); *Kingan* (Cy Kendall).

Gold Is Where You Find It has somehow slipped into movie obscurity, and undeservedly so. It is a prime example of cinematic Americana of its day, which is to say it shines with optimism about the American experience and supports the ethics of work and honesty. It also does it in the lush, original three-strip Technicolor process, which may not have been true to life but nonetheless made even the simplest visual facts more attractive. The film has the added virtue of presenting Olivia de Havilland to the world for the first time in Technicolor.

While many pictures have been made about the California gold rush of 1849, few have looked at life in the Sacramento Valley thirty years after John Sutter made his staggering discovery. In the years following the Civil War—the era of this handsome movie—the valley's mining activities grew as engineering developments made progress ever more feasible, while at the same time the region blossomed into the vast agricultural belt it is today. Hence the conflict of this particular plot, which follows the inevitable fight between the miners (by 1879 almost all corporation

With George Brent

controlled) and the farmers. The hydraulic equipment used by the miners tear up the picturesque slopes and hillsides and send rocks, subsurface soil, and debris down into the farmlands and interfere with the richness of the topsoil.

With Claude Rains

Jared Whitney (George Brent) is a vital, dynamic engineer sent from San Francisco to supervise the mining operations. He meets Serena Ferris (Olivia) after saving her young brother Lance (Tim Holt) from being beaten in a barroom brawl, and he falls in love with her. She is the lively daughter of the valley's most prominent citizen, Colonel Ferris (Claude Rains), who is also the leader of the farming faction. He organizes the valley farmers and gets a court injunction against the mining company. Whitney now finds himself ordered by his bosses to continue operations in defiance of the injunction. He refuses but hastens to the scene of the conflict in order to prevent bloodshed. Whitney is unable to stop the battle, in which Lance is brutally killed, but he manages to bring it to a halt by blowing up a dam, which unleashes a torrent of water that washes all the participants away from their barricades. After the waters have subsided, Whitney opts for the life of a gentleman farmer, with Serena as his bride. Justice is on their side, as a judge warns all that "the land is for the people . . . its fruits are precious and exhaustible—may it survive its spoilers." Big business loses the day.

Gold Is Where You Find It was largely filmed on location, around Perris, California, the site of its historically accurate story. Director Michael Curtiz's expertise with action sequences is well in evidence, as is Sol Polito's appreciative color photography of the fine landscapes and Max Steiner's rhapsodic score. Among the actors, Claude Rains easily walked away with top notice for his portrayal of the fearless Colonel Ferris. On the other hand, any farmer or miner who came across a lovely, spirited lass like Olivia's Serena would have found a prize truly worth fighting for.

With Tim Holt and George Brent

With George Brent

With Harry Davenport and
Tim Holt

On the set with George Brent
and Margaret Lindsay

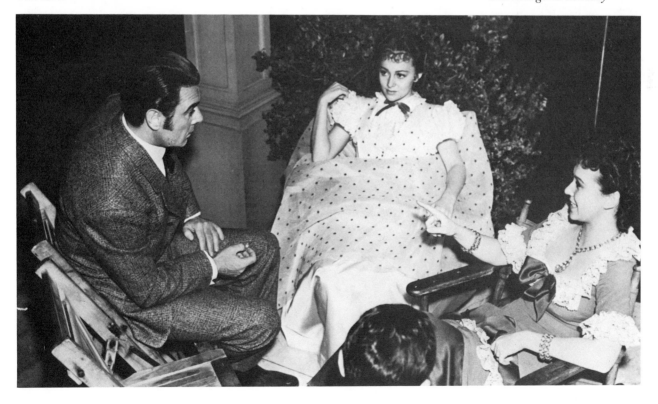

THE ADVENTURES OF ROBIN HOOD

1938
A Warner Bros. First National Picture,
Produced by Hal B. Wallis,
Directed by Michael Curtiz and William Keighley,
Written by Norman Reilly Raine and Seton L. Miller,
Photographed in Technicolor by Sol Polito and Tony Gaudio,
Music by Erich Wolfgang Korngold,
102 minutes.

CAST:

Sir Robin of Locksley (Errol Flynn); *Maid Marian* (Olivia de Havilland); *Sir Guy of Gisbourne* (Basil Rathbone); *Prince John* (Claude Rains); *Will Scarlet* (Patric Knowles); *Friar Tuck* (Eugene Pallette); *Little John* (Alan Hale); *High Sheriff of Nottingham* (Melville Cooper); *King Richard* (Ian Hunter); *Bess* (Una O'Connor); *Much the Miller's Son* (Herbert Mundin); *Bishop of the Black Canons* (Montagu Love); *Sir Essex* (Leonard Willey); *Sir Ralf* (Robert Noble); *Sir Mortimer* (Kenneth Hunter); *Sir Geoffrey* (Robert Warrick); *Sir Baldwin* (Colin Kenny); *Sir Ivor* (Lester Matthews); *Dickon Malbete* (Harry Cording); *Captain of Archers* (Howard Hill); *Kent Road Tavern Proprietor* (Ivan Simpson).

Warner Bros. spent a great deal of effort, time, and money—their biggest budget until then—on making *The Adventures of Robin Hood* and it was obvious to everyone involved that the picture would be a winner. But none of them could predict that it would shape up into just about the most perfectly realized adventure film ever made. It is one of the few instances in the history of films where the fine parts actually add up to an even finer whole. The screenplay by Norman Reilly Raine and Seton I. Miller is literate and witty, and Michael Curtiz' direction (with portions done by William Keighley) gives it buoyancy and precise pacing. The costumes of Milo Anderson and the sets of Carl Jules Weyl (for which he won an Oscar) fairly glow in the Technicolor photography of Sol Polito and Tony Gaudio, the two Trojan cameramen at Warners for so many years. The score by Erich Korngold (his second Oscar winner) radiates from the picture and the casting is faultless.

Errol Flynn might well have been Robin Hood in another life and, as Maid Marian, Olivia de Havilland looks as if she has stepped out of a storybook, making her a perfect match for Flynn. Basil Rathbone's arrogant

Sir Guy of Gisbourne, with eloquent, biting diction, is a masterpiece of screen villainy, as is Claude Rains' sly, epicene Prince John. Alan Hale as Little John, Eugene Pallette as Friar Tuck, Patric Knowles as Will Scarlet, Melvile Cooper as the cowardly High Sheriff of Nottingham, and Ian Hunter as the noble King Richard—all are fondly memorable figures.

With Errol Flynn, Eugene Pallette, and Basil Rathbone

The script draws mostly from legend and its historical value is slight. The setting is England during the reign (1189–1199) of King Richard I, at a time when he was held for ransom by King Leopold of Austria, having been captured on his way home from the Third Crusade. In his absence his brother Prince John elects himself Regent and conducts a brutal campaign to subjugate the English, mostly Saxons, in order to conduct a dictatorship for himself and his fellow Norman knights. Sir Robin of Locksley thinks otherwise and organizes the populace of Nottinghamshire to revolt. He makes known his plans when he unexpectedly turns up at the Prince's banquet at Nottingham Castle. After laying down his own laws, Robin escapes and joins his band of outlaws in Sherwood Forest. It is at the banquet that Robin sees for the first time the lovely Lady Marian Fitzwalter, the ward of King Richard. He is impressed with her beauty but she is anything but impressed with his apparent treason.

Robin next sees Marian when he and his men ambush the Norman columns headed by Sir Guy and the High Sheriff as they transport the huge amount of ransom money to London. Supposedly collected, by harsh taxation, to free the King, it is actually bound for the private Norman

Make-up break, with Flynn and Eugene Pallette

With Melville Cooper and Basil Rathbone

110

coffers—that is, until Robin diverts it in the right direction. He and his men entertain their captives and Robin gradually makes Marian see the justice of his cause. He shows her some of the badly injured peasants, who have been tortured by the Normans and robbed of all they owned. She is impressed with his dedication, "But it's lost you your rank, your lands . . . made you a hunted outlaw when you might have lived in comfort—security. What's your reward for all this?" Robin looks surprised, "My reward? You just don't understand, do you?" Marian is somewhat embarrassed by his question, "I'm sorry. Yes, I do begin to see . . . a little . . . now." Robin replies, "If that's true . . . then I want no greater reward." By the time they part they are in love, a fact which does not go unnoticed by the High Sheriff. Having been set free by Robin, he and Gisbourne return to Nottingham where they suggest to Prince John that he stage an archery tournament, with the first prize being given by Maid Marian. Robin is, of course, the winner but he underestimates the Normans and becomes their captive.

Robin is sentenced to be hanged and it is Marian who organizes his escape from the gallows. She goes to a tavern she knows is frequented by Robin's men and, once having convinced them of her sincerity, she tells them the way in which Robin may be helped. The plan is a success and some time later, one evening, he climbs the castle wall to arrive at her window to tell her how grateful he is. He arrives as she and her maid (Una O'Connor) are discussing the subject of love. He is clearly the reason for the discussion, although she tries to deny it. Their banter proves that they are equally in love with each other, which leads her to be concerned about his present safety: "You are leaving here—at once. Please, darling! Every minute you're here you're in danger—you've got to go now." Robin asks her to come with him. She agrees but then reasons it is better for her to stay: "I could help more by watching for treachery here and leaving you free to protect Richard's people, till he returns." Robin, heartened by her love, agrees and leaves.

King Richard and his group of Crusaders return to England and join forces with Robin to bring Prince John's ambitions to an end. In the meantime, Gisbourne, suspecting that she is in league with Robin, arrests Marian and takes her before John. The Prince tells her she will be sorry she interfered. "Sorry? I'd do it again—if you killed me for it!" John looks at her with a wry grin: "A prophetic speech, my lady . . . for that is exactly what is going to happen to you." The astonished Marian points out that only a king can condemn her to death and he rejoins by telling her that within two days he will be king.

John's coronation, set up on the assumption that Richard is dead, is demolished by Robin, Richard, and their men, who sneak into the ceremony disguised as monks. Gisbourne meets his end after a lengthy (and marvelously filmed) sword fight with Robin, after which Richard asks him if there is anything he can do for the outlaw who showed him his

With Patric Knowles, Alan Hale, and Eugene Pallette

With Harry Cording, Alan Hale, and Basil Rathbone

duty toward his country. Robin requests and receives a pardon for his men. "But is there nothing for yourself?" Robin glances toward the radiant Marian and the King understands. He asks her, "And do you, too, wish . . . ?" She beams. "More than anything else in the world, sire." Richard restores Robin to knighthood and to his lands and adds several new titles, including Earl of Sherwood and Nottingham. "My first command to you, my Lord Earl, is to take in marriage the hand of the Lady Marian. What say you to that, Baron of Locksley?" After the cheering subsides, Robin gives his reply: "May I obey all your commands with equal pleasure, sire."

Surely no adventure movie could have a better ending than that—and surely no one could have been a better Robin Hood than Flynn. It is the apex of his career and no matter how tragic his eventual decline, it is impossible to dim the 1938 image of him dashing about Sherwood Forest and Nottingham Castle, a truly merry rogue in battle and charming when in love. A large slice of that glory is shared with Olivia de Havilland, an exquisite Maid Marian, portraying a substantial human being in her own right. Marian is gentle and dignified but firm and loyal. She is no mere bystander. Once she understands Robin's cause and once she gives her heart to him, she is a participant in his life. She risks that life leaving the castle to give his men her plan for his escape from the gallows and she boldly speaks up when on trial. Marian is a lady with courage and she is a vital factor in Robin's success—all of which is clearly and beautifully delineated by Olivia. It would not be the same film without her.

With Errol Flynn

Like most other actors who went from picture to picture in those golden days, Olivia never dwelt much on any one of them and it did not dawn upon her until many years later just how fine a film *Robin Hood* is. She went to see it in Paris in the summer of 1959 and wrote a letter to Flynn telling him how impressed she was and that she had rather dismissed the picture in the past. "An apology twenty years late. But I tore it up. I reconsidered, deciding Errol would think I was silly. I'll always be sorry. A few months later he was dead. Seeing *Robin Hood* after all these years made me realize how good all our adventure films were, and I wrote Errol that I was glad I had been in every scene of them. I was astounded by *Robin Hood's* vitality, its effervescence. I thought it was simply wonderful. It was a revelation to me. It was classic."

*With amateur
cinematographer Basil
Rathbone*

With Errol Flynn

FOUR'S A CROWD

1938
A Warner Bros. Picture,
Produced by Hal B. Wallis,
Directed by Michael Curtiz,
Written by Casey Robinson and Sig Herzig, based on a story by
    Wallace Sullivan,
Photographed by Ernest Haller,
Music by Heinz Roemheld,
91 minutes.

CAST:

Robert Kensington Lansford (Errol Flynn); *Lorri Dillingwell* (Olivia de Havilland); *Jean Christy* (Rosalind Russell); *Patterson Buckley* (Patric Knowles); *John P. Dillingwell* (Walter Connolly); *Silas Jenkins* (Hugh Herbert); *Bingham* (Melville Cooper); *Preston* (Franklin Pangborn); *Herman* (Herman Bing); *Amy* (Margaret Hamilton); *Butler Pierce* (Joseph Crehan); *Young* (Joe Cunningham); *Buckley's Secretary* (Dennie Moore); *First Lansford Secretary* (Gloria Blondell); *Second Lansford Secretary* (Carole Landis); *Mrs. Jenkins* (Reine Riano); *Dr. Ives* (Charles Trowbridge); *Charlie* (Spencer Charters).

Of the eight films Olivia de Havilland made with Errol Flynn, the least memorable is *Four's a Crowd*. Flynn, even at this stage of his career, was beginning to get a little weary of the swashbuckling image and constantly badgered Warners for Cary Grant-like comedies. With *Robin Hood* a smash hit, it seemed a good commercial ploy to let the stars romp through a light-headed farce and prove their versatility. *Four's a Crowd* is certainly light-headed. Flynn comes off best, playing a glib, enterprising public relations man, but Olivia is required only to once again play the dizzy, love-prone rich girl. Their fans must have been puzzled at Warners' decision to again have Olivia end up in the arms of Patric Knowles rather than those of Flynn.

Flynn's role as Robert Kensington Lansford was roughly based on the career of an almost legendary PR man, Ivy Ledbetter Lee, who died in 1934 after having blazed publicity history with his colorful campaigns for such famous clients as the Rockefeller family. The main thrust of *Four's a Crowd* is Lansford's desire to snare John P. Dillingwell (Walter Connolly) as a client. Dillingwell is a blustering eccentric who is not only one of the richest men in America but also one of the most hated. His image is atrocious, and Lansford reasons that if he can alter that image his acclaim in the PR business will be limitless. To this end he has his girl friend Jean (Rosalind Russell) persuade newspaper owner Patterson Buckley (Patric Knowles) to get him his old job back as the editor of the paper. Jean is a leading reporter for the paper and willing to help Lansford use it for his whitewashing of the cantankerous Dillingwell.

Another reason for Lansford getting his job back, which he does, is that Buckley is engaged to Dillingwell's granddaughter Lorri (Olivia). Dillingwell dotes on Lorri and Lansford begins to romance her, which gives him access to Dillingwell's well-guarded estate. Since Dillingwell is also a toy train enthusiast, with a vast miniature railroad in his backyard, Lansford pretends to be a fellow enthusiast and thus becomes a friend of the surly millionaire. His plans start to strain with the resentment of both Buckley and Jean over his playing up to Lorri, who shows signs of falling in love with the dashing publicist. Jean comes across some damaging information about Dillingwell, which Buckley would like to publish, and in order to get it he suggests they rush off and get married. Hearing about this Lansford rushes to the same marriage parlor with Lorri. When all the arguments die down and the four of them come to their senses, they revert to their former partners. Lansford marries Jean and Buckley marries Lorri. And nothing is published about Dillingwell, good or bad.

Four's a Crowd was intended only as pleasing, passing product and as such it came close to reaching its mark. It did little for the careers of its four stars, although Flynn proved a certain flair for comedy, especially in the scene where he runs for his life down the Dillingwell driveway, pursued by a pack of large, ferocious dogs. In his scenes with Olivia he several times refers to her as a "nitwit," from which it may be gathered it is not a role high in her filmography.

With Patric Knowles, Rosalind Russell, and Errol Flynn

With Walter Connolly and
Rosalind Russell

With Errol Flynn and
Walter Connolly.

With Melville Cooper and
Walter Connolly

HARD TO GET

1938
A Warner Bros. Picture,
Produced by Hal B. Wallis,
Directed by Ray Enright,
Written by Jerry Wald, Maurice Leo, and Richard Macauley,
based on the story *Classified* by Stephen Morehouse Avery,
Photographed by Charles Rosher,
Songs by Harry Warren and Johnny Mercer,
Music direction by Leo F. Forbstein,
80 minutes.

CAST:

Bill Davis (Dick Powell); *Margaret Richards* (Olivia de Havilland); *Big Ben Richards* (Charles Winninger); *Roscoe* (Allen Jenkins); *Connie Richards* (Bonita Granville); *Case* (Melville Cooper); *Henietta Richards* (Isabel Jeans); *John Atwater* (Thurston Hall); *Hattie* (Penny Singleton); *Stanley Potter* (Grady Sutton); *Schaff* (John Ridgely); *Burke* (Jack Mower); *Judge Harkness* (Granville Bates); *Mrs. Atwater* (Nella Walker); *Butler* (Sidney Bracy); *Maid* (Lottie Williams); *Chauffeur* (Herbert Evans).

Dick Powell had been Warners' most popular singing star all through the early and mid-Thirties, but by 1938 his appeal was starting to wane. By then Warners had decided that the era of lavish musicals, with big casts and gargantuan choreography by Busby Berkeley, was over, and Powell himself had long since tired of starring in them. He wanted meatier material and the chance to prove himself as something other than a crooner. Some years later he would indeed prove himself an actor, but the chance never came from Warners Bros. Instead they put him into light comedies, with a song here and there, until his contract ran out in late 1938, at which time he made a fast exit from the studio, never to return.

Hard to Get is a fairly amusing piece of material, with Powell showing more spine than his previous roles allowed. It obviously seemed a good idea to co-star him with Olivia de Havilland and reunite the lovers of *A Midsummer Night's Dream*. The pairing worked well, although it offered Olivia nothing much more than a continuation of her spoiled-rich-girl characterizations of *It's Love I'm After* and *Four's a Crowd*. Here she is perhaps just a little bit more spoiled and much more willful. Her *Hard to Get* character of Margaret Richards is a young lady who believes that merely having a lot of money is sufficient passport to anywhere. She meets an immovable object in Bill Davis (Powell) when she drives her convertible into his gas station-motel, fills the tank, and then finds she isn't carrying any cash. He makes her work off the debt by cleaning out some of his motel cabins.

Margaret resents Bill and plans her revenge. He is an ambitious fellow who has designed an auto court for a proposed chain of them across the country. What he badly lacks is money and one of the financiers he would like to see is Big Ben Richards (Charles Winninger), who just happens to be Margaret's father. She keeps that fact from him but gives him the password that will get him in to see her father, knowing that he hates ambitious young men and will throw Bill out on his ear. He does. Then she poses as a maid in her own home and invites Bill to visit her. Again he is thrown out. He persists in his visits to the Richards' office, getting in each time by pretending to be a window cleaner, a scrub woman, and a telegraph boy, always with his blueprints but always getting bounced. Hearing about a ball being given at the Richards' mansion, Bill turns up as a musician in blackface. He happens to hear Margaret boasting of what she has done to him and he leaves in anger, so angry that he drops his blueprints and storms out. The prints come to the attention of Big Ben, who thinks them wonderful. A chain of auto courts—just what he had in mind. Who's the designer? Where is he? Margaret now realizes she loves Bill Davis and that he will make a great son-in-law for Big Ben.

Hard to Get is not hard to take, although the film displays an almost contemptuous attitude toward the wealthy set. Charles Winninger steals all his scenes as the daffy, physical fitness-mad tycoon, who delights in besting his put-upon valet (Melville Cooper). Powell handles his role with ease and Olivia is fun to watch as the girl who makes life frenetic for him—until love takes over. The most memorable sequence in the picture is the canoe ride on the lake in Central Park, when Powell sings one of the great Harry Warren songs to her, "You Must Have Been a Beautiful Baby" (lyrics by Johnny Mercer).

With Allen Jenkins and Dick Powell

With Charles Winninger and Melville Cooper

With Penny Singleton

With Dick Powell

With Allen Jenkins

WINGS OF THE NAVY

1939
A Warner Bros. Cosmopolitan Picture,
Produced by Lou Edelman,
Directed by Lloyd Bacon,
Written by Michael Fessier,
Photographed by Arthur Edeson,
Aerial photography by Elmer Dyer,
Music direction by Leo F. Forbstein,
88 minutes.

CAST:

Cass Harrington (George Brent); *Irene Dale* (Olivia de Havilland); *Jerry Harrington* (John Payne); *Scat Allen* (Frank McHugh); *Commander Clark* (John Litel); *Lieutenant Parsons* (Victor Jory); *Prologue Speaker* (Henry O'Neill); *Dan Morrison* (John Ridgely); *Lieutenant White* (John Gallaudet); *Instructor* (Regis Toomey); *Instructor* (Don Briggs); *Ted Parsons* (Edgar Edwards); *Armando Costa* (Albert Morin); *Commandant* (Jonathan Hale); *Captain March* (Pierre Watkin).

With George Brent

Wings of the Navy is such a dated movie that its main value now is that of research material for anyone looking into the machines and methods of American naval aviation in early 1939. It also serves as a reminder that Hollywood was quite active, obviously with military encouragement, in gearing up the American public to the realization that its armed forces needed expansion in the light of what was going on in Europe. The sentiment of films like this one was very much a pre-call to arms, with life in the services presented as adventurous and inviting. However, for Olivia de Havilland the picture was nothing very much. Almost any young actress could have filled its meager distaff functions.

Warner Bros. received Navy Department cooperation in filming at the air stations in Pensacola, Florida, and San Diego, California, and apparently limitless use of personnel in showing the training of air cadets and the new kinds of land and sea planes involved. Balancing the seriousness of purpose with the banter of service cameraderie, plus a little romance, the thin story line of *Wings of the Navy* concerns two brothers, one a veteran naval aviator, Cass Harrington (George Brent), and the other, the much younger Jerry (John Payne), who transfers to the air service after being discontented with his experiences in the submarine branch. Both are devoted navy men, as was their father. Cass loves a young lady named Irene Dale (Olivia), but after she meets Jerry her interest begins to

With John Payne and George Brent

change course.

The film follows Jerry's course of instruction at Pensacola as he is put through the paces of the latest developments in naval aviation. After graduation he is posted to San Diego for further training in the handling of the huge PBY-2 sea-going bombers and the various tactics of blind flying, formation bombing, and defence. In the meantime Cass is injured in a crash and leaves the Navy in order to devote himself to designing planes for naval warfare. In order to test fly his brother's newest design and prove its worth to the Navy, Jerry also leaves the service. But with the success of the tests he is reinstated and assigned to duty in Honolulu. Realizing that Jerry and Irene are in love, the older brother gracefully steps aside and wishes them well.

One of the more memorable things about *Wings of the Navy* is its stirring theme song, "Wings Over the Navy," written by Harry Warren and Johnny Mercer. The song and all the splendid photography of planes in formation probably inspired many young men to join the Naval Air Service. If so, the film served its purpose. The one member of the enterprise who felt it didn't serve her purposes very well was Olivia, who was beginning to worry that her career was actually losing altitude.

With George Brent, John Payne, and Frank McHugh

With George Brent and John Payne

128

With George Brent

DODGE CITY

1939
A Warner Bros. Picture,
Produced by Hal B. Wallis,
Directed by Michael Curtiz,
Written by Robert Buckner,
Photographed in Technicolor by Sol Polito,
Music by Max Steiner,
104 minutes.

CAST:

Wade Hatton (Errol Flynn); *Abbie Irving* (Olivia de Havilland); *Ruby Gilman* (Ann Sheridan); *Jeff Surratt* (Bruce Cabot); *Joe Clemens* (Frank McHugh); *Rusty Hart* (Alan Hale); *Matt Cole* (John Litel); *Dr. Irving* (Henry Travers); *Colonel Dodge* (Henry O'Neill); *Yancey* (Victor Jory); *Lee Irving* (William Lundigan); *Tex Baird* (Guinn "Big Boy" Williams); *Harry Cole* (Bobs Watson); *Mrs. Cole* (Gloria Holden); *Munger* (Douglas Fowley); *Mrs. Irving* (Georgia Caine); *Surrett's Lawyer* (Charles Halton); *Bud Taylor* (Ward Bond); *Mrs. McCoy* (Cora Witherspoon); *Orth* (Russell Simpson); *Barlow* (Monte Blue).

Admirers of the handsome, Technicolored super western *Dodge City* may be surprised to hear it referred to by Olivia de Haviland as just about the nadir in her film career. This is not so much a comment on the picture itself but a lament on the limited role it offered her, at a time when she was getting worried about what seemed like a decline in her professional image. Having fun with *Four's a Crowd,* after the great impact of *Robin Hood,* was nothing to worry about, but following that rather mild comedy with *Hard to Get* and *Wings of the Navy* was not the progress for which she yearned. Reading the script of *Dodge City* only added to her depression, since it gave her no chance to establish anything other than a nice, pretty presence as a girl with whom the rambling, adventurous hero (Errol Flynn) finds he can start a new life.

Dodge City was one of a number of big-budget westerns Hollywood produced in 1939—others being *Stagecoach, The Oklahoma Kid, Jesse James, Union Pacific,* and *Frontier Marshall*—as the industry found profit in epic Americana. All of them depicted western history in somewhat glossy terms and combined simplistic moral values with exciting action in splendid outdoor settings. This was also the film which, to his surprise, made a western star of Flynn. His refined British accent and demeanor are here explained by presenting him as an Irishman, whose adventures include serving with the British Army in India and the Confederate cavalry in the Civil War. That there was nothing noticably Irish about Flynn, other than his name, did not seem to bother either Warner Bros. or the multitudes of Flynn fans. The success of *Dodge City* lead to his being assigned to other westerns and an eventual reference by Flynn to himself as a kind of rich man's Roy Rogers.

The expansive, stately title music by Max Steiner sets up the picture as an epic tale about the founding of a town during the lustiest, bloodiest years of the frontier. A pioneering railroad engineer, Colonel Dodge (Henry O'Neill), forges his rails to a point in Kansas to meet the cattle drives coming up from Texas. A community grows up around this point and when someone asks what it should be called, one of the colonel's employees, a trail blazer named Wade Hatton (Flynn), suggests the obvious name, "Dodge City." Hatton and his chums, Rusty (Alan Hale) and Tex (Guinn "Big Boy" Williams) then find work as wagon guides and the town rapidly grows into a fierce mixture of business and pleasure. With plenty of money and hordes of wild cowboys continually arriving and leaving, the town develops as a trigger-happy, boozy hell-hole, largely controlled by Jeff Surrett (Bruce Cabot).

Hatton becomes a wagon master to a party which includes Abbie Irving (Olivia) and her undisciplined brother Lee (William Lundigan). The bored Lee takes to shooting off his pistol in order to create some

With Errol Flynn

With William Lundigan

132

excitement, despite having been warned by Hatton that the shots are likely to stampede the accompanying herd of cattle. On one occasion the drunken Lee defies Hatton, who has to fire a shot at the young man to disarm him, hitting him in the knee. But the shot sets off a stampede and Lee is trampled to death. The horrified Abbie refuses to see the circumstances and tells Hatton she despises him as a murderer. Later, in Dodge City, Hatton pays his respects and sympathies to Doctor and Mrs. Irving (Henry Travers and Georgia Caine), who understand Hatton's actions and forgive him. The doctor comments that Dodge City has become brutally wild and needs good men like Hatton, but the Irishman is more interested in further adventures than in settling down. However, in time he manages to charm Abbie and they begin going out together. She becomes the assistant to the town's newspaper editor (Frank McHugh) and on Sundays becomes a Sunday school teacher.

The editor is relentless in exposing Surrett and his gang, until one of them, Yancey (Victor Jory), murders him. Abbie decides to continue the newspaper by herself, with Hatton looking out for her safety. Later, when a youngster (Bobby Watson) is accidentally killed in the street, due to drunken brawling by cowboys, Hatton accepts the job of sheriff and conducts a tough and successful campaign to clean up the town. He also learns that Yancey was responsible for killing the newspaper editor. Hatton takes Yancey away to a nearby town in order to see that Surrett

With Errol Flynn and Frank McHugh

133

cannot interfere with justice, but Surrett and his men take over the train in which Hatton is travelling. Unknown to Hatton, Abbie is also on the train, on her way to visit relatives. It is Abbie who spots the Surrett forces and warns Hatton and Rusty. Surrett isolates Hatton, Rusty, and Abbie in the mail car and sets fire to it. Rusty spots an axe and uses it to smash a way out of the car to the engine, from which point Hatton uses a rifle to bring down Surrett and Yancey as they gallop away.

Dodge City ends with Abbie setting out with Wade Hatton as his wife, bound for adventures further west—in Virginia City, Nevada, to be exact. Such an ending made a follow-up film inevitable. However, when *Virginia City* was made a year later, it had nothing to do with the characters in *Dodge City* and actually took place during the Civil War, a decade prior to the action in the previous picture. Olivia was not required to be the heroine; the role of the Confederate lady spy who falls in love with the northern officer (Flynn) went to Mariam Hopkins, who was seven years older than Flynn and turned out to be the least well-paired of his leading ladies.

Of her role as Abbie Irving, Olivia has little comment other than that she was bored for the most part and generally felt that she was only one step ahead of a nervous breakdown. "I was in such a depressed state that I could hardly remember the lines." However, as depressed as working on *Dodge City* might have been for her, the film remains a solidly entertaining, albeit rather square-in-concept, western, invigorated by Michael Curtiz' direction and containing the most glorious, protracted, elaborately choreographed barroom brawl in the history of the movies. The film advanced Flynn's popularity and helped put him in the Top Ten at the box office in 1939, the only year he reached that august upper echelon. Olivia may have ended the picture in a state of despair but she had little time thereafter to ponder. A very, very big upward turn was about to lift her career into the firmament of film lore.

On location with one of the clumsy but magnificent old Technicolor cameras

With Errol Flynn

GONE WITH THE WIND

1939
A David O. Selznick Picture, released by MGM,
Directed by Victor Fleming,
Written by Sidney Howard, based on the novel by Margaret
   Mitchell,
Photographed in Technicolor by Ernest Haller,
Music by Max Steiner,
229 minutes.

CAST:

Rhett Butler (Clark Gable); *Scarlett O'Hara* (Vivien Leigh; *Ashley Wilkes* (Leslie Howard); *Melanie Hamilton* (Olivia de Havilland); *Mammy* (Hattie McDaniel); *Gerald O'Hara* (Thomas Mitchell); *Mrs. O'Hara* (Barbara O'Neill); *Aunt Pittypat Hamilton* (Laura Hope Crews); *Dr. Meade* (Harry Davenport); *Belle Watling* (Ona Munson); *Suellen O'Hara* (Evelyn Keyes); *Careen O'Hara* (Ann Rutherford); *Prissy* (Butterfly McQueen); *India Wilkes* (Alicia Rhett); *Big Sam* (Everett Brown); *Uncle Peter* (Eddie Anderson); *Charles Hamilton* (Rand Brooks); *Frank Kennedy* (Carroll Nye); *Mrs. Merriwether* (Jane Darwell); *Maybelle Merriwether* (Mary Anderson); *Emmy Slattery* (Isobel Jewell); *Jonas Wilkerson* (Victor Jory); *Bonnie Blue Butler* (Cammie King); *Bonnie's Nurse* (Lillian Kemble); *Tom* (Ward Bond); *Yankee Deserter* (Paul Hurst); *Brent Tarleton* (George Reeves); *Stuart Tarleton* (Fred Crane).

At one point in *Gone With the Wind,* its fiery heroine Scarlett O'Hara refers to her faithful friend Melanie as a "pale faced, mealy-mouthed ninny." Much later, after Melanie has died, Rhett Butler gives his opinion. "She was the only completely kind person I ever knew." As sketched by authoress Margaret Mitchell, Melanie was a frail, shy young lady with a heart-shaped face, rather plain but possessing a certain sedate dignity and inner strength. After reading the book, Olivia de Havilland made up her mind that Melanie was the character she wanted to play. Many actresses vied for the role of Scarlett and many were considered. In discussing GWTW with her boss Jack Warner, once he had agreed to the loan-out, he told her to go after Scarlett and forget Melanie. She replied that she had no interest in Scarlett. She *had* to play Melanie. She understood the part. She could be everything Mitchell had in mind, and as for sedate dignity and inner strength . . . any close associate of the actress could testify to those qualities.

In a letter* to Daniel T. O'Shea, the Vice-President of Selznick International, dated November 18, 1938, David O. Selznick wrote: "I would give anything if we had Olivia de Havilland under contract to us so that we could cast her as Melanie..." Later in the same letter he says, "Warners have so far definitely refused to consider letting us have de Havilland for Melanie, but I think they might be persuaded, especially if we offer them (Paulette) Goddard in trade, since I understand Jack Warner thinks well of Goddard. This would mean giving a star making role to a Warner player, but it looks as though we may be stuck, in which case we may want to break our necks to get de Havilland..."

With Leslie Howard

Had *GWTW* been an entirely MGM production, as Louis B. Mayer hoped, the part of Melanie would have gone to Maureen O'Sullivan. Since Selznick wanted to run his own show without outside influence, he decided otherwise. Among those considered for Melanie were Geraldine Fitzgerald, Andrea Leeds, Anne Shirley, and Priscilla Lane. But between Selznick's determination and Olivia's determination, things could only go one way. Jack Warner tried to bring Selznick into his camp by offering him Bette Davis as Scarlett and Errol Flynn as Rhett, but Davis refused to be a part of that team, much as she wanted the role. Warner showed no interest in promoting Olivia's career and refused to let her be loaned to Selznick. Fortunately, Mrs. Anne Warner sided with Olivia and was able to bring enough pressure to bear to change his mind.

Another firm ally for Olivia at this time was the man Selznick assigned to direct his mammoth picture, George Cukor. When Cukor suggested to Joan Fontaine that she would be a good choice for Melanie, Fontaine said the part did not interest her. Like most actresses in Hollywood at that time she felt she was Scarlett, but she thought that her sister would be just right as Melanie. After a reading with Olivia, Cukor more than agreed and took her to see Selznick, who then went after Jack Warner. Cukor was shortly thereafter fired by Selznick, who thought his style not sufficiently vigorous, and replaced him with Victor Fleming, Unbeknownst to Selznick, both Olivia and Vivien Leigh consulted with Cukor all through the production of *GWTW* on how to play their roles. Gable had been responsible for bringing in his virile friend Fleming but neither actress thought him sensitive enough for their needs. Recalls Cukor, "After I left the picture, Olivia would come over to my house to do some moonlighting with me—I'd run over the scenes with her, and so on. She felt rather guilty about going behind Vivien's back, until she found out that Vivien was doing exactly the same thing, too."

With Leslie Howard and Vivien Leigh

The directing of *GWTW* became even more strained when Fleming collapsed under pressure and Sam Wood was brought in to direct some of the sequences. Selznick was cautious about revealing who directed what, but it is known that Wood directed the sequence of the Yankee de-

*Memo from David O. Selznick. Edited by Rudy Behlmer. Viking, 1972.

serter being shot by Scarlett on the stairs of Tara, in which the sick Melanie lends a helping hand, and the massive sequence with the hundreds of Confederate wounded at the Atlanta railroad depot. In this hodgepodge of directorial styles, the two actresses were grateful for the support of Cukor.

Olivia's role was strained somewhat by the attitude of Leslie Howard. Much as she was dedicated to her part, Howard made no secret that he thought his role as Ashley was that of a soft dullard and that he was playing it only because of the money. Many people thought that the part should have gone to Randolph Scott, a genuine Virginia gentleman.

The "wind" in Margaret Mitchell's epic yarn was the Civil War and that which was "gone" in its wake was the plantation aristocracy of the Old South, along with its gentility and its wealth. Whether it was ever quite the land of cavaliers, elegant manners, and contented slavery as painted by Mitchell is grandly beside the point. *GWTW* was not intended by either the authoress or by David O. Selznick as an historical document. The film opens up at Tara, the plantation home of Gerald O'Hara (Thomas Mitchell) and his wife Ellen (Barbara O'Neill). Of their three daughters, Scarlett (Vivien Leigh) is by far the prettiest, the most willful, and the most determined. So much so that Suellen (Evelyn Keyes) and Careen (Ann Rutherford) are constantly jealous and simpering. Scarlett is determined to marry Ashley Wilkes (Leslie Howard), but as much as he is attracted to the spirited beauty, he prepares to marry his cousin Melanie Hamilton (Olivia), a girl of quiet charm and grace. Out of spite and also to stop gossip about her obvious interest in Ashley, Scarlett marries Melanie's brother Charles (Rand Brooks), who immediately has to leave her because war breaks out and he is called to the colors. He is also called to an early grave.

Scarlett's pretended grief makes no impression on Rhett Butler (Clark Gable), an adventurer and gambler from Charleston who spots Scarlett as the same kind of person as himself—selfish and rather ruthless. He falls in love with her but realizes he cannot rid her of her continuing passion for Ashley. He goes off to war, not as a soldier but as a privateer, blockade runner, and profit maker. As such he is a man apart from the fervent patriotism and the gradually declining resources of the South. He next meets Scarlett when he visits Atlanta as Sherman's forces approach the city. Bored with life at Tara, Scarlett has gone to live with Melanie and help Aunt Pittypat (Laura Hope Crews) take care of her as the frail but staunch Melanie awaits the birth of her baby. Both she and Scarlett work as nurses as thousands of Confederate wounded and dying pour into the city. By the time Melanie gives birth, Atlanta is in a state of chaotic siege and it is only through the help of Rhett that she and Scarlett are able to get out of the city. With only a rickety wagon, an exhausted horse and an almost demented servant (Butterfly McQueen), Scarlett arrives back at Tara, to find the estate in ruin, her mother dead and her father in a state of mental decline.

The determined Scarlett vows never to be needy again. She takes over the running of the plantation and by marrying a devoted admirer who also happens to own a lumber mill (Carroll Nye) she gets herself back into money and power. Ashley returns from the war and stays at Tara with Melanie. Scarlett's husband dies, which gives her command of his assets. Rhett Butler comes back into her life and she finally accepts his offer of marriage, more in recognition of his virility and prestige than because of any real love for him. He in time hopes for a change in her but becomes disgusted with her perpetual infatuation with Ashley.

Scarlett and Rhett have a daughter, Bonnie Blue (Cammie King), who is adored by her father, who finds in the child the love he cannot get from his wife. When Bonnie Blue is killed in a fall from her pony, Rhett is himself almost destroyed. He sits for days in grief at the deathbed of his daughter. The gentle Melanie, now an ailing woman, comes to him and persuades him to allow for the funeral and also to take care of Scarlett, who needs him. A short while later Melanie dies. The way is clear for Scarlett to go after grieving Ashley, but now she sees him as a weak man whose strength rested largely with his love for Melanie. She realizes the true wealth of her life is Rhett, but he is long tired of her and leaves their home. When she asks, "What's to become of me?" he replies, "Frankly, my dear, I don't give a damn." But Scarlett is not a woman to ever give up. She knows there is always tomorrow.

With Vivien Leigh and Ona Mun.

With Leslie Howard, Laura Hope Crews, and Mary Young

Gone With the Wind's immediate success and its continuing success through the years are too well known to need further comment. It remains one of the few films to win both high critical approval and the devotion of the public. It also did not go unnoticed at the Academy Award presentations on the evening of February 29, 1940, at the Los Angeles Ambassador Hotel. It was voted the Best Film of 1939 and Oscars also went to scenarist Sydney Howard (who died in an accident in August of that year, while the film was still in production); to Vivien Leigh as Best Actress; to Hattie McDaniel as Best Supporting Actress; to Victor Fleming as Best Director; to Hal C. Kern and James E. Newcom as Best Film Editors; to Lyle Wheeler as Best Art Director; and to Ernest Haller and Ray Rennahan as Best Color Cinematographers. David O. Selznick was at the same time given the Irving Thalberg Award. It was on this occasion that Bob Hope first served as the Master of Ceremonies for the Oscars. During his opening monologue he referred to the dominance of *GWTW* over the evening. "What a wonderful thing, this benefit for David Selznick."

Olivia de Havilland was nominated for an Oscar as Best Supporting Actress but lost to Hattie McDaniel. It was a bitter loss, since she had worked so hard for so long on Melanie (*GWTW* was half a year in production), but years later Olivia realized the importance involved in McDaniel winning the award. They were friends and they worked together several times again. But there was no lack of appreciation for Olivia within the

With Clark Gable and Ward Bond

industry, or with the critics or with the public. Hers was a perfectly realized characterization, just as Margaret Mitchell had intended and well in tune with the similar perfection struck by Leigh as Scarlett and Gable as Butler. Seldom has a film been better cast, in almost every role, thanks to a relentlessly driving producer who would not settle for second best.

But for the skill and subtlety of Olivia's playing, the role of Melanie could easily have sunk into that of a nice but dull secondary character. It has never been easy to play a thoroughly good-hearted, well-behaved role and have the character seem vital and interesting. Melanie as written is almost incapable of believing that there is any bad in anyone. She is naive about human behavior, but she also has a strength that rises to any occasion. She seems either unaware or strangely sympathetic about Scarlett's obsession with Ashley. Perhaps she realizes how badly Ashley needs her. But it is Melanie, always frail, who volunteers as a nurse during the terrible siege of Atlanta, and whose goodness gives her the strength to survive an exhausting pregnancy and the rough trip to Tara. She is there to back Scarlett after the killing of the Yankee looter, and it is Melanie who speaks with compassion to prostitute Belle Watling and accepts her money to help "the cause." It is Melanie who comforts the grieving Rhett, not his wife, and it is she who tells Rhett to be kind to Scarlett. But most of all, and throughout the whole story, Melanie is the perfect counterbalance to the driving, conniving Scarlett. Melanie's composure is the calming influence on Scarlett's rage to live. The characterizations also point up how very, very different two women can be.

Olivia has said that the tender, compassionate Melanie is her favorite role and that "she is the woman I wish I could be." The success of the portrayal, its depth and texture, suggests that there must surely be much of the one lady in the other.

With Vivien Leigh

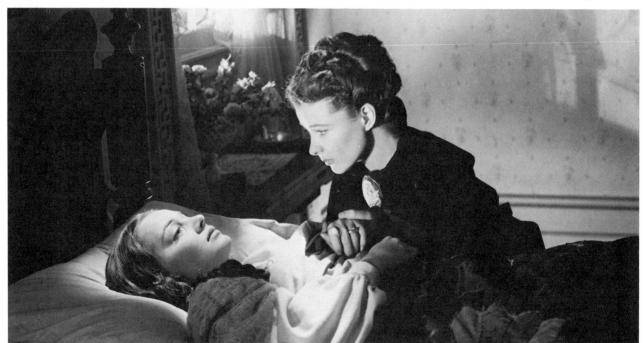

With Clark Gable

THE PRIVATE LIVES OF ELIZABETH AND ESSEX

1939
A Warner Bros. First National Picture,
Produced by Hal B. Wallis,
Directed by Michael Curtiz,
Written by Norman Reilly Raine and Aeneas MacKenzie, based on
    the play *Elizabeth the Queen* by Maxwell Anderson,
Photographed in Technicolor by Sol Polito,
Music by Erich Wolfgang Korngold,
106 minutes.

CAST.

Queen Elizabeth (Bette Davis); *Earl of Essex* (Errol Flynn); *Lady Penelope Gray* (Olivia de Havilland); *Francis Bacon* (Donald Crisp); *Earl of Tyrone* (Alan Hale); *Sir Walter Raleigh* (Vincent Price); *Lord Burghley* (Henry Stephenson); *Sir Robert Cecil* (Henry Daniell); *Sir Thomas Egerton* (James Stephenson); *Margaret Radcliffe* (Nanette Fabray); *Lord Knollys* (Ralph Forbes); *Lord Mountjoy* (Robert Warrick); *Sir Edward Coke* (Leo G. Carroll).

Although it was released at the end of November, 1939, a few weeks prior to *Gone With the Wind*, *The Private Lives of Elizabeth and Essex* was made while the Selznick picture was being put together, with Olivia de Havilland returning to Warners within days of completing her role as Melanie. It was not a joyous return. Any thoughts that her work on *GWTW* might lead Jack Warner to promote her with first-rate starring vehicles were crushed when he assigned her to third billing in this Bette Davis–Errol Flynn historical pageant. It was a name-below-the-title role and, because of her previous standing as a popular Flynn co-star, the assignment was a painful one.

Flynn claimed that this was his least favorite film, a view brought about because of his having to take second billing in what would surely be a Bette Davis triumph. Never a secure actor, he was thoroughly intimidated by Davis, who made it known she did not want him as Essex and begged Jack Warner to get Laurence Olivier for the part. Since Olivier was not "box office" and Flynn was his top hero-actor, there was no way Warner would alter his casting. He was aware that the Maxwell Anderson play *Elizabeth the Queen* was a dialogue tour-de-force (it had starred Lynn Fontanne and Alfred Lunt on Broadway), and he reasoned that to turn it

With Errol Flynn

147

into a movie it needed all the glamour he could inject into it, including having scenarists Norman Reilly Raine and Aeneas MacKenzie write in some outdoor sequences.

Whether as a play or a film, *Elizabeth and Essex* is a romantic fantasy with only a hazy connection to historical fact. It is unlikely that the Queen and Robert Devereaux, the Earl of Essex, were actually lovers as depicted by Anderson. He certainly was a great favorite of hers and he dallied with her affections, but Essex was thirty-four when beheaded in 1601; she was sixty-eight and died two years later. Essex was, as Anderson realized, a vainglorious, conceited, attractive young man ever bent on gaining power and constantly irritating his queen with his gauche ways of getting it. The film opens with Essex's triumphal entry into London after his spectacular sacking of the city of Cadiz, a battle which makes him a hero in the eyes of the public but not in those of Her Majesty. Instead of honoring him at court, as he expected, she humiliates Essex by pointing out that the Spanish sank their treasure ships rather than let them fall into his hands, and what the crown needs is money, not empty glory. His shame is deepened when she immediately appoints Sir Walter Raleigh (Vincent Price) to high office, making him Essex's superior. The two men are rivals for power and Essex storms out of the court to sulk at his country home at Wanstead.

Among the many Essex admirers is the Queen's chief lady-in-waiting, Lady Penelope Gray (Olivia). Neither her love for him nor her advice to be careful in dealing with the monarch are heeded by the headstrong Essex. His friend Francis Bacon (Donald Crisp), a respected advisor to the queen, manages to affect a reconciliation between the two and Essex returns to court. Despite their attempts to be understanding lovers, his vanity and her pride cause constant squabbles. She knows that what he really wants is to be king and rule England with her on equal terms, terms which she realizes are impossible . She warns him that her court is rife with intrigue and that there are others who want power and control. Chief among them are Raleigh, Robert Cecil (Henry Daniell), and Lord Burghley (Henry Stephenson), who are eager to get Essex out of the court. They spot their opportunity when news comes that the Irish are in revolt and that a military campaign is needed to quell them. At a council meeting they subtly goad Essex into accepting the challenge to settle the business in Ireland. The Queen is sickened by the obvious duping of Essex but knows he cannot be stopped once his courage and military skill is questioned.

In Ireland Essex is defeated by the brilliant tactics of the Earl of Tyrone (Alan Hale), who admits that things might have been different had Essex been properly backed by his queen. The furious Essex is puzzled by the lack of supplies and by the lack of communication with Elizabeth. Neither she nor Essex are aware that their letters have been intercepted and destroyed by Cecil and his cohorts, and that Lady Penelope has been tricked into being a part of the conspiracy. She had only hoped to break up the romance and perhaps win Essex for herself. When she demures in her allegiance to the plotters, Cecil warns her, "You have a lovely head and neck, milady. It would be a pity to separate them."

Despite his defeat in Ireland, Essex is still a popular figure with the English masses and on his return to London he and his loyal forces take over the palace at Whitehall. The Queen seems to give in to his wishes and meekly invites him to take her throne. Once she agrees to share the crown, he dismisses his men, whereupon Elizabeth turns on him and has him arrested. Despite her love, she will not let England fall into his hands. Essex is sent to the Tower of London and after he refuses Elizabeth's offer to compromise, to become her consort, he goes to his death on the block.

Elizabeth and Essex benefits from magnificent sets and costumes, and a richly heraldic, romantic score by Korngold, but it fails to realize its potential. It is very much a Davis vehicle, with Flynn appearing ill-at-ease, except in one scene—and that is with Olivia, their only scene together in the film. Penelope warns Essex about the dangers of being in love with a queen and that she wished he loved her instead. For the length of this short scene, Flynn seems comfortable, as indeed he should be with an actress with whom he had long had a close rapport, but when the Queen interrupts the scene, Flynn-Essex returns to being uncomfortable. Much more effective are those scenes between Davis and Olivia. Lady Penelope is divided between her love for Essex and her undoubted loyalty to Elizabeth. She has the courage to occasionally taunt her monarch about loving a younger man; in one scene they play chess together and Penelope improves her position with every move. But Elizabeth sweeps the board with her hand and demonstrates where *real* power lies. In another scene Penelope and another favorite lady-in-waiting, Margaret (Nanette Fabray), entertain their queen with a duet, a song cunningly selected by Penelope to ridicule the love of an older woman for a young man. As the lyrics unfold Elizabeth begins to stir, and when Penelope gets to the lines., "But could youth last, and love still love, had joys no date, nor age no need..." Elizabeth explodes in fury, smashes every mirror within range and tongue lashes Penelope as "a brazen wench . . . a shameless hedge drab. . . . " Penelope's balloon of courage is quickly deflated.

Despite her few good scenes in this beautifully worded but rather stuffy epic, Olivia did not enjoy being a part of *The Private Lives of Elizabeth and Essex*. In order to work for Selznick, she had promised Jack Warner to be good and do as he asked, but she feels "he was provoking me to break my word to him and be just what he'd said I would be, which was difficult. It was very hard for me to make *Elizabeth and Essex*, I was really miserable, but I did it because I had given him my word."

With Bette Davis, Vincent Price, Henry Daniell, and Donald Crisp

150

With Nanette Fabray

RAFFLES

1940
A Samuel Goldwyn Picture, released by United Artists,
Directed by Sam Wood,
Written by John Van Druten and Sidney Howard, based on the
  novel *The Amateur Cracksman* by E. W. Hornung,
Photographed by Gregg Toland,
Music by Victor Young,
71 minutes.

CAST:

A. J. Raffles (David Niven); *Gwen Manders* (Olivia de Havilland); *Lady Kitty Melrose* (Dame May Whitty); *Mackenzie* (Dudley Digges), *Bunny Manders* (Douglas Watson); *Lord George Melrose* (Lionel Pape); *Barraclough* (E. E. Clive); *Harry Crawshay* (Peter Godfrey); *Maud Holden* (Margaret Seddon); *Bingham* (Gilbert Emery); *Wilson* (Hilda Plowright); *Butler* (Vesey O'Davoren); *Footman* (George Cathrey); *Merton* (Keith Hitchcock); *Umpire* (Forrester Harvey); *Cabbie* (James Finlayson); *School Mistress* (Elspeth Dudgeon).

With David Niven

Jack L. Warner may not have been willing to help Olivia de Havilland's career at his own studio by giving her worthwhile roles, but he was well aware of her stock as a commodity because of the success of *Gone With the Wind*. He now loaned her to Samuel Goldwyn in order to get Joel McCrea as the star of Warners' *Espionage Agent*. Olivia had given Warner her word that she would not be difficult after working for Selznick (she had promised him that in order to get the role of Melanie), so she dutifully turned up at the Goldwyn lot and reported to director Sam Wood. Her feelings about the Goldwyn assignment were negative, believing that this re-make of the successful Ronald Colman version of 1930 could not be an improvement and that her part had no substance or challenge.

Raffles was David Niven's twenty-second film but the first in which he received top billing. Goldwyn had put him under contract in 1935 and used him as either a bit player in Goldwyn product or as a loan-out player, by which means he actually made a profit on Niven. In the Spring of 1939 Goldwyn thought it was time to give the twenty-nine-year-old Scotsman the star treatment and possibly turn him into another Colman. Apart from the fact that the film did not have the impact Goldwyn sought, it finished shooting just as war broke out in Europe and Niven immediately left to join the British army. Goldwyn found this patriotic fervor a little strange for an actor on the edge of stardom but he prom-

*With Dudley Digges and
David Niven*

153

ised to hold his contract open for the duration. Niven was gone for six years but Goldwyn was as good as his word.

The Niven *Raffles* is virtually a duplicate of the Colman *Raffles*. The two films are within a minute of the same length. Goldwyn brought in John Van Druten to touch up the Sidney Howard script of 1930, but Sam Wood was so tired from *Gone With the Wind* that he obviously looked at the Colman version and copied the set-ups. Wood was, in fact, called back by the demanding Selznick from time to time and became so exhausted that he asked William Wyler to step in and help direct some of the concluding scenes with Niven. The end result was a fairly pleasing comedy-thriller, with Niven being amusingly flippant as the gentleman crook, A. J. Raffles, a man with a reputation as a top flight cricketer and society blade, who steals jewels in order to help needy friends. By 1940 this kind of material was already starting to seem old hat. Indeed, the E. K. Hornung novel had spawned a successful play and two early movie versions. John Barrymore played *Raffles* in 1914 and House Peters did it in 1925.

Raffles is a man who enjoys playing cat-and-mouse with the police and often steals *objets d'art* simply to stir up trouble at Scotland Yard and then return the items. Hearing that his friend Bunny Manders (Douglas Walton) is in serious debt, Raffles gets himself invited for the weekend to

With E. E. Clive, Douglas Walton, Lionel Pape and David Niven

the home of Lord and Lady Melrose (Lionel Pape and Dame May Whitty), in order to crack their safe and steal a valuable necklace. His plan to give the necklace to Bunny and have him redeem it for the reward goes awry when a real thief (Peter Godfrey) gets wind of the scheme and lifts the necklace. He is apprehended by Raffles, who takes the necklace and turns the crook over to Inspector Mackenzie (Dudley Digges), who has wisely been on hand all the time, knowing that something like this was bound to happen. He releases the crook, knowing he will follow Raffles to his home and try to get the necklace. By the time the inspector arrives at Raffles' apartment in London, Raffles has paid off the crook and handed the necklace to Bunny to redeem. He also agrees to reform, due to the love of Bunny's sister Gwen (Olivia).

Raffles is a good example of the "English" movies that used to be turned out by Hollywood quite regularly and were populated by the once-thriving British colony of actors in California. Two of them, the superb character players Dame May Whitty and Dudley Digges, easily steal all the scenes from the star players, including Olivia, whose part is so thin it defies playing. She knew it at the outset. "I had nothing to do with that English scene, I had nothing to do with that style of film and I was nothing to that part the way it was written."

With Douglas Walton and David Niven

With Peter Godfrey and David Niven

MY LOVE CAME BACK

1940
A Warner Bros. Picture,
Produced by Wolfgang Reinhardt,
Directed by Curtis Bernhardt,
Written by Ivan Goff, Robert Buckner, and Earl Baldwin, based on
   a story by Walter Reisch,
Photographed by Charles Rosher,
Music by Heinz Roemheld,
81 minutes.

CAST:

Amelia Cullen (Olivia de Havilland); *Tony Baldwin* (Jeffrey Lynn); *Dusty Rhodes* (Eddie Albert); *Jo O'Keefe* (Jane Wyman); *Julius Malette* (Charles Winninger); *Mrs. Malette* (Spring Byington); *Paul Malette* (William Orr); *Valerie Malette* (Ann Gillis); *Ludwig* (S. Z. Sakall); *Dr. Kobbe* (Grant Mitchell); *Dr. Downey* (Charles Trowbridge); *Dowager* (Mabel Taliferro); *Butler* (Sidney Bracy); *Sophie* (Nanette Vallon).

My Love Came Back might well be titled *Olivia Came Back—to What?* It isn't that it is a bad picture but it isn't the kind of vehicle an actress who had made a solid impression on both the critics and the public in *Gone With the Wind* would expect to be handed on her return to her home studio. *My Love Came Back* is a genial little comedy that would have been a good showcase for a starlet needing screen exposure, such as Olivia had been five years previously. Still, it was better than the other pictures Warners offered her after her *GWTW* accolades, and after months of being on suspension it was better to work than not.

Here Olivia is a talented but highly strung young violinist named Amelia Cullen at the Brissac Academy in New York. She flings a book through a glass door when her teacher (S. Z. Sakall) reprimands her for being late. The book hits the principal (Grant Mitchell), who demands an explanation and discovers that Amelia has to give lessons because she is supporting her mother. Brissac students are not supposed to give lessons, which means Amelia is likely to be expelled. The situation comes to the attention of kindly Julius Malette (Charles Winninger), who tells the principal he will supply Amelia with a scholarship provided his name is not mentioned. Julius runs a music company and accepts the presidency of Brissac Academy, thereby assuring that Amelia, whom he secretly admires, will continue her education.

Things turn sour when Julius' grown-up children (William Orr and

Ann Gillis) find out that their father is supporting Amelia. They suspect that she is his mistress, and they also resent his turning over the music company to his manager, Tony Baldwin (Jeffrey Lynn). When she learns about Julius subsidizing her, Amelia moves to return the scholarship check. But the situation is greatly worsened by the desperate need for money of her friends Dusty (Eddie Albert) and Joy (Jane Wyman), both fellow music students and both intent on starting their own orchestra. They forge Amelia's name on the returned check in order to pay their dues with the musicians' union. At the same time they persuade Amelia to join the band, whose gimmick is the swinging of the classics.

The band's first engagement turns out to be at the home of Julius Malette, who delights in now leading his children to think that the scholarship money actually comes from Tony Baldwin. In the meantime, Amelia and Tony meet at the Beaux Arts ball and fall in love. When she turns up to play the engagement at the Malette house, Amelia faints with surprise. Mrs. Malette takes her aside and learns the truth about the mix-up. Dusty explains to Tony about his having stolen the check which Amelia tried to return, and he also repays the money. The Malette children understand. The orchestra is a hit and the Brissac principal even decides that the new swing music should be a part of the curriculum. And thus *My Love Came Back* whirls its light-headed way to its conclusion.

With Jane Wyman (next to Olivia) and Eddie Albert (at the piano)

With Charles Winninger

With Eddie Albert

SANTA FE TRAIL

1940
A Warner Bros. First National Picture,
Produced by Hal B. Wallis,
Directed by Michael Curtiz,
Written by Robert Buckner,
Photographed by Sol Polito,
Music by Max Steiner,
110 minutes

CAST:

Jeb Stuart (Errol Flynn); *Kit Carson Halliday* (Olivia de Havilland); *John Brown* (Raymond Massey); *George Armstrong Custer* (Ronald Reagan); *Tex Bell* (Alan Hale); *Bob Halliday* (William Lundigan); *Rader* (Van Heflin); *Jason Brown* (Gene Reynolds); *Cyrus Halliday* (Henry O'Neill); *Windy Brody* (Guinn "Big Boy" Williams); *Oliver Brown* (Alan Baxter); *Martin* (John Litel); *Robert E. Lee* (Moroni Olsen); *Phil Sheridan* (David Bruce); *Barber* (Hobart Cavanaugh); *Major Sumner* (Charles D. Brown); *Kitzmiller* (Joseph Sawyer); *James Longstreet* (Frank Wilcox); *Townley* (Ward Bond); *Shoubel Morgan* (Russell Simpson); *Jefferson Davis* (Erville Alderson).

Santa Fe Trail is one of the more peculiar entries in the listing of western movies. In the first place it is barely a western at all, being an historical drama set up as an action-packed adventure movie, and it has nothing to do with the actual Santa Fe trail. Instead it is the story of the early years of cavalryman J. E. B. Stuart, played by Errol Flynn in his usual slightly mock-heroic style, and Stuart's involvement with abolitionist John Brown, played in Satanic, florid manner by Raymond Massey. Robert Buckner's script contains some strange errors, among them the graduation of a half-dozen famed Civil War generals from West Point in 1854, Stuart being the only one who graduated that year. Buckner makes George Armstrong Custer (Ronald Reagan) a fellow graduate and close friend of Stuart's, even though Custer was a boy in 1854 and never met Stuart. Buckner paints John Brown as a demented, rather villainous idealist, while somehow both condoning the need for the abolitionist movement and the government's need to stamp it out.

Viewed as an examination of a vital time in American history, *Santa Fe Trail* is indeed a strange motion picture. Viewed as a piece of entertainment it is rattling good fun, with director Michael Curtiz whipping it along and Warner expertise visible on every hand. The female lead in such a film might well expect to sink into the background but here the

reverse is true. Olivia de Havilland's role as Kit Carson Halliday is vital and interesting, although the character is pure invention on the part of Robert Buckner. Jeb Stuart, a Virginia gentleman, actually married a lady of his own social level in that state. Still, he would not have done badly for himself had he married Kit Carson Halliday, a spirited young lady with a mind of her own. There is barely any comparison between Olivia's Kit and her role as Abbie in her previous Flynn western *Dodge City*. This is a much more lively and confidant lady, both in regard to screen image and private circumstances.

Prior to the graduation at West Point in 1854, there are rumblings of coming political trouble. A malcontent cadet, Rader (Van Heflin), berates the aristocratic Stuart for his class distinction in the South and the ownership of slaves. Cashiered as a trouble maker, Rader joins the forces of John Brown as a military adviser. Following their graduation, Stuart and Custer are sent as lieutenants to serve with the 2nd US Cavalry at Fort Leavenworth, Kansas. Part of their job is to guard wagon trains and commercial shipments heading westward in the direction of the Sante Fe trail (which actually began in Missouri) and to generally guard the frontier in the face of turmoil caused by the pro- and anti-slave factions. It is on one of these missions that Stuart and Custer come into conflict with Brown, who poses as a shipper of Bibles. When a dropped crate spills out rifles, the soldiers go into action and one of Brown's sons is killed in the skir-mish. It becomes obvious that Brown and his followers are waging a campaign in Kansas—towns are burned, people killed, and ranches sacked—and the army steps up its counter-measures.

With William Lundigan, Henry O'Neill, Ronald Reagan, Errol Flynn and William Marshall

With Ronald Reagan and Errol Flynn

When not engaged in their frontier patrols, Stuart and Custer vie for the affections of Kit, who is the daughter of Cyrus Halliday (Henry O'Neill), the owner of a freight line. Kit, so named because her father was a friend of scout Kit Carson, is no shrinking violet. She helps manage her father's business and she tomboyishly strides around the freight yards assigning men to their work. She takes an amused attitude toward the flirtations of the two lieutenants but with time succumbs to the love of Stuart, while trying to let Custer down lightly. Later she manages to introduce him to a lovely friend (Susan Peters) and the problem is solved.

The conflict between Brown and the government comes to a head at Harpers Ferry, West Virginia, in 1859, when the abolitionist forces seize the town and make its arsenal their fortress. Rader, who has deserted Brown because he has not been paid, warns the army of Brown's intentions to seize greater control and march on Washington. A force of cavalry and marines under the command of Colonel Robert E. Lee (Moroni Olsen) is despatched to Harpers Ferry and Stuart is instructed to approach Brown under a flag of truce and seek his surrender. The fanatic Brown scoffs at such a gesture and triggers off the battle which brings his career to an end. Arrested and tried, he is hanged as Stuart, Kit, Custer, Lee, and the others stand by as glum witnesses. An officer remarks, "So perish all such enemies of the Union," a rather dubious point of view in light of Brown's cause to free the slaves. This dramatically downbeat scene is alleviated, but none too successfully, by an immediate segue to

With Errol Flynn

With Alan Hale

the marriage of Stuart and Kit on a train. As the end titles appear over the receding train, Max Steiner's forceful score ends the film with a paraphrase on "John Brown's Body." Perhaps Steiner's final musical point says what the film cannot openly express: "John Brown's body lies a mouldering in the grave but his soul goes marching on."

Sante Fe Trail is clearly a split level movie, on the one hand a controversial treatment of history, good enough to trigger serious discussion, and on the other hand an exciting adventure yarn brought off with panache by Curtiz, his players, and his handsome production facilities. Scenarist Buckner may have been confused in his political focus but he had the sense to make Olivia's role a pivotal one in balancing the mixed values. It is Kit Carson Halliday who doubts the government actions, while disapproving of Brown's bloody tactics. She has a firm, clear vision of what is going on, quite apart from controlling the attentions of her soldier boy swains, and when they think that the turmoil has blown over once Brown has been quelled, she knows differently. She predicts there is more trouble on the way, most probably a civil war. Rather surprisingly for a Flynn adventure romp, the leading lady is someone of real substance. It is an interesting role and Olivia's performance gives it flesh-and-blood dimensions. And her provocative, slightly tongue-in-cheek manner makes it easy to understand why any frontier lieutenant would be driven to hope for her hand.

With Flynn and director
Michael Curtiz (left)

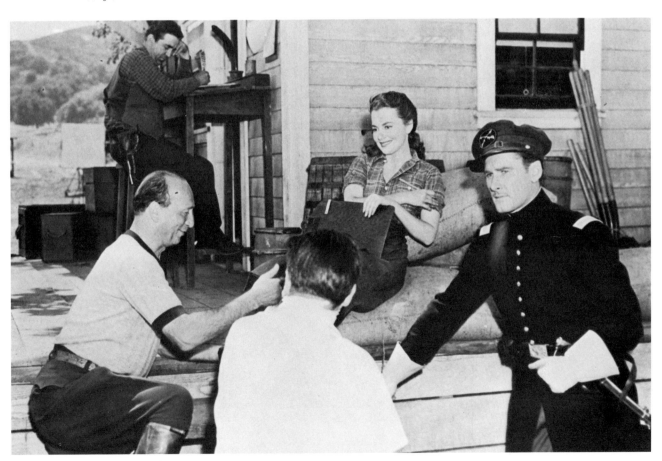

THE STRAWBERRY BLONDE

1941
A Warner Bros. First National Picture,
Produced by Jack L. Warner and Hal B. Wallis, Associate Producer
    William Cagney,
Written by Julius and Philip Epstein, based on the play *One Sunday
    Afternoon* by James Hagan,
Photographed by James Wong Howe,
Music by Heniz Roemheld,
97 minutes.

CAST:

Biff Grimes (James Cagney); *Amy Lind* (Olivia de Havilland); *Virginia Brush*
(Rita Hayworth); *Old Man Grimes* (Alan Hale); *Nick Pappalos* (George
Tobias); *Hugo Barnstead* (Jack Carson); *Mrs. Mulcahey* (Una O'Connor);
Harold (George Reeves); *Harold's girl* (Lucille Fairbanks); *Big Joe* (Edward
McNamara); *Toby* (Herbert Heywood); *Josephine* (Helen Lynd); *Bank
President* (Roy Gordon); *Street Cleaner Foreman* (Tim Ryan); *Official*
(Addison Richards); *Policeman* (Frank Mayo); *Bartender* (Jack Daley); *Girl*
(Susan Peters); *Baxter* (Frank Orth); *Inspector* (James Flavin); *Sailor*
(George Campeau).

In her concern to find more interesting material than the roles Warners offered her, Olivia de Havilland took to sneaking scripts out of the studio and reading them at home in the hope of finding something worthwhile. It was in this manner that she discovered and decided upon the part of Amy Lind, a free-thinking, turn-of-the-century nurse in *The Strawberry Blonde*. Since the part called for a rather plain woman, of the kind that would later become known as a *feminist,* it was not one her employers would have considered her for. But Olivia saw its potential and easily convinced William Cagney, who had acquired the property for his brother James, to cast her in it. It was an ideal vehicle for the appealingly feisty Cagney, who by now had managed to achieve quite some say in the choice of material he would make at Warners. In this regard he was head and shoulders above most of the Warner stars, who either accepted their assignments or went on suspension. Ann Sheridan decided that the title role offered her little challenge and opted for suspension, at which Warners borrowed the upcoming Rita Hayworth from Columbia.

The Strawberry Blonde was a re-make of *One Sunday Afternoon*, which Paramount had made in 1933 with Gary Cooper playing the leading role of Biff Grimes, a quick-tempered, ex-convict who pulls himself together with the aid of his wife Amy and becomes a success after taking a correspondence course as a dentist. It was not a part within Cooper's range and the film quickly sank from sight. On the other hand it was precisely within Cagney's range. And its sentimental basis was beautifully abetted by the masculine, fast-paced style of director Raoul Walsh. Seven years later Warners called upon Walsh to make the picture again, as a musical with Dennis Morgan as Biff and reverting to the original title, but it sadly lacked the sparkle of the Cagney version.

The story opens with Biff as a small but successful New York dentist who gets a call from building contractor Hugo Barnstead (Jack Carson) to pull a tooth. Biff accepts the job with a controlled sense of anger. It was Barnstead who was responsible for Biff going to jail and it was he who stole Biff's sweetheart, the gorgeous Virginia Brush (Rita Hayworth), a strawberry blonde. Flashback: Biff and Hugo are chums but rivals for the attention of Virginia, who brings along her friend Amy (Olivia) when the quartet have a date. Amy asserts herself as a modern-thinking girl, quite open in her regard for men and given to winking and clicking her teeth when she agrees with an opinion or when stating her own forthright views. Biff makes a little headway with Virginia but she soon decides to

With James Cagney

With Rita Hayworth, James Cagney and Jack Carson

marry the brash Hugo, who is a go-getter in his business plans. Somewhat on the rebound Biff courts and eventually marries Amy, and finds her to be more vulnerable and softly feminine than her manner had led him to believe. She is, in fact, a fine and understanding wife.

Hugo makes Biff a vice-president in his construction company, a job Biff does not understand, since all he has to do is sign papers. Unwittingly he becomes a stooge for Hugo's shady dealings and when one of the Barnstead projects collapses due to the use of inferior building materials, it is Biff who finds himself the culprit and who goes to jail for five years. With the loving support of Amy, Biff studies his correspondence course in dentistry and after completing his sentence he returns home and picks up his life. Later, when Hugo comes to him as a patient, Biff is tempted to kill him with gas but settles instead on merely pulling out a tooth without the use of gas. What really changes Biff's attitude toward the contemptible Hugo is the observation that he has become a henpecked, reviled husband. The "strawberry blonde" of Biff's infatuation

With George Tobias and James Cagney

has become a nagging shrew, and he is suddenly aware of his good fortune in winning the loving Amy.

Olivia was wise in deciding to play Amy in this charming, period comedy-drama. It was different from anything she had previously done and revealed her talent for combining the qualities of good-heartedness and lovingness in portraying such a woman. Also, the slight awkwardness she had shown in her early comedies had by now settled down into a pleasant confidence, with quite some skill in conveying a refined sense of naughtiness. *The Strawberry Blonde* met with fine response from both the critics and the public, and a good deal of praise for her contribution. The reviewer for *Time* called the picture a "blithe, sentimental, turn-of-the-century buggy ride. Cagney makes the hero a tough but obviously peachy fellow. But the strawberry humdinger, Rita Hayworth, takes the picture away from him, and dark-eyed Olivia de Havilland, with her electric winks, each followed by a galvanizing 'Exactly!' takes it away from both of them."

With George Tobias and James Cagney

With Jack Carson, James Cagney, and Rita Hayworth

With James Cagney

HOLD BACK THE DAWN

1941
A Paramount Picture,
Produced by Arthur Hornblow, Jr.,
Directed by Mitchell Leisen,
Written by Charles Brackett and Billy Wilder, based on the novel by
   Ketti Frings,
Photographed by Leo Tover,
Music by Victor Young,
115 minutes.

CAST:

Georges Iscovescu (Charles Boyer); *Emmy Brown* (Olivia de Havilland); *Anita Dixon* (Paulette Goddard); *Van Den Luecken* (Victor Francen); *Inspector Hammock* (Walter Abel); *Bonbois* (Curt Bois); *Berta Kurz* (Rosemary De Camp); *Josef Kurz* (Eric Feldary); *Flores* (Nestor Paiva); *Lupita* (Eva Puig); *Christine* (Micheline Cheirel); *Anni* (Madeleine LeBeau); *Tony* (Billy Lee); *Mechanic* (Mikhail Rusumny).

Hold Back the Dawn is not a great film but it is a good one and very important in the career of Olivia de Havilland. It enabled her to break out of the restrictive casting at Warners and play a role quite different from anything she had previously tried. The role is that of an ordinary, decent, virginal young woman from a small town whose life and sexuality is awakened by a suave European, whose own life is in turn changed for the better by her. With her portrayal of Emmy Brown in this skillfully written, near-tragic romance, Olivia was playing a truly believable, flesh-and-blood woman instead of a storybook heroine. It resulted in an Oscar nomination as Best Actress, which she lost to sister Joan for *Suspicion*. More importantly it resulted in greater prestige.

Charles Brackett and Billy Wilder had Olivia in mind for the part of Emma, but they knew it would take subterfuge to get her from Jack Warner, who still showed no signs of promoting her career. They also knew he never loaned any of his players unless he needed someone. The actor Warner wanted at this time was Paramount's Fred MacMurray, to co-star with Errol Flynn in *Dive Bomber*, but the Paramount executives played it very cool when Warner read the list of his available talent. They made no reaction to the mention of Olivia's name, but some days later called Warner to say that she would *do*, since they had to have *somebody* in order to start production. Thus Warner was tricked into giving them precisely the actress they wanted and at no direct cost.

Much of the pleasure of making *Hold Back the Dawn* came from working with director Mitchell Leisen, a gentleman of excellent taste, who treated actors with more deference than Olivia had received from any director at Warners, and whose background included drawing and set decoration. In short, Leisen was a consummate artist. He was also a good actor on occasion. The film begins at Paramount, as a former Rumanian dancer and ladies' man named Georges Iscovescu (Charles Boyer) visits Leisen on the set of *I Wanted Wings,* as he directs a scene with Veronica Lake and Brian Donlevy. Iscovescu has known the director from a European meeting and tells him he will sell him a good, true story for five hundred dollars. Leisen realizes the man is in earnest and he agrees to listen. Flashback.

Iscovescu is one of a number of Europeans living in a Mexican border town, all of them hoping to get into the United States after having fled their Nazi-ravaged homelands. Many of them find entry difficult because their nationality quotas are full. In the case of Iscovescu, it may take eight years to qualify for entry. A former dancing partner, Anita (Paulette Goddard) advises him of a way to get around the immigration restrictions, and that is by marrying an American. She had married and then

quickly divorced a jockey in order to cross the border. One day Iscovescu spots Emmy, a teacher from Azusa, who is conducting a group of her pupils on a Mexican visit. He gets her to stay at his hotel overnight and in the morning tells her he loves her. It takes little of his expert charm to steer her into marriage.

Emmy takes the children back to Azusa, while he applies for his immigration papers. The radiant Emmy returns and they leave for a week of driving around in her car on a honeymoon trip. She is such a warm and trusting girl that Iscovescu feels shame for his duplicity and fakes an injury to his shoulder in order to avoid consummating the marriage. Once back in the border town, Anita tells Emmy about the man she has married, about his reputation as a gigolo, and the reason for the marriage. Any doubts she has about the story are destroyed by a knowing immigration official (Walter Abel), who tells her it is an everyday occurrence. Deeply offended, Emmy faces her husband and tells him, "I live in a small town and we eat at the drugstore but we leave a tip just the same. The lies I told were not too much to pay for one week's happiness. But let me go." Her lies are those told to the immigration officials, about how she was marrying him for love and that she knew all about his background.

Emmy leaves Mexico in anger and drives furiously home, so furiously that she loses control of her car and becomes badly hurt in an accident. Iscovescu learns of this and, after crossing the border illegally, makes his way to her hospital. He tells her of his genuine love and respect and that he will not take advantage of her. In doing so he gives Emmy the will to

With Charles Boyer

live. He then proceeds to Paramount where he convinces Leisen to buy his story. The immigration officer (Abel) arrives at this time and escorts Iscovescu back to Mexico, where he assumes he is doomed to stay.

Iscovescu gives his payment from Leisen to Emmy's hospital. The immigration official is impressed by the transformation in the man's character and decides he will not list Iscovescu's illegal entry into America. Some weeks later Emmy arrives at the border and waves to Iscovescu. They run toward each other as the sympathetic immigration official looks on approvingly.

Hold Back the Dawn tells a compassionate story. The original material was supplied by Ketti Frings, based on her own experiences in getting her husband Kurt into the country from Mexico. Kurt later became a Hollywood agent and numbered Olivia among his clients. In less firm and tasteful hands than those of Mitchell Leisen the material might have become maudlin, dealing as it does with people whose lives are in the balance. Aside from the excellent performances of Olivia and Boyer, the picture contains an effective performance by Rosemary De Camp as a pregnant woman who gains entry by slipping across the border to have

With Paulette Goddard

her child born American. Also impressive is Victor Francen as a Dutch professor who acts as a father figure to the stranded Europeans. They reside in a dreary hotel called the Esperanza and Leisen poignantly sets it up as a kind of way station in No Man's Land. Leisen handles them all with respect, as he does the Mexican setting. To his credit, there are no caricatures in *Hold Back the Dawn*.

Of her co-star, Olivia says, "It was a pleasure to work with Charles Boyer. I always felt such rapport with him." Her feelings of respect for the actor were actually a hindrance at the start of production. In the initial scenes where Iscovescu is trying to impress Emmy, she is supposed to affect disinterest, but Olivia's regard for Boyer clearly showed in her eyes and Leisen asked her to do the scenes again some days later. It was not until years later that she found out the reason for the re-takes.

In the opinion of *The New York Times* reviewer, Bosley Crowther, "Olivia de Havilland plays the school teacher as a woman with romantic fancies whose honesty and pride are her own—and the film's chief support."

In working with Mitchell Leisen, Olivia found herself being given more guidance than she had received in a long time. In his book *Hollywood Director* (Curtis Film Series, New York, 1972), David Chierichetti interviewed Olivia about working with dialogue coach Phyllis Loughton, who assisted Leisen on most of his films and who also functioned as a talent adviser at Paramount: "It was hard for me to get used to working with Phyllis at first. I hadn't had much detailed direction since Max Reinhardt on *A Midsummer Night's Dream,* and I resented it a bit. We had dialogue directors at Warners but they just listened to you read the lines to check on pronunciation of the words. They didn't get into the characterizations either. They blocked out the action and from then on, you were on your own, for better or worse. That was what I was used to, but I knew I could learn something from Phyllis, so I kept still. She did help me; Emmy Brown is a good performance and I'm proud of it. But Mitch was the director of the picture. Phyllis didn't usurp his function, she just complemented it, helping us to find more depth and dimension."

With Walter Abel and Charles Boyer

With Paulette Goddard and director Mitchell Leisen

THEY DIED WITH THEIR BOOTS ON

1942
A Warner Bros. First National Picture,
Produced by Hal B. Wallis,
Directed by Raoul Walsh,
Written by Wally Kline and Aeneas MacKenzie,
Photographed by Bert Glennon,
Music by Max Steiner,
140 minutes.

CAST:

George Armstrong Custer (Errol Flynn); *Elizabeth Bacon Custer* (Olivia de Havilland); *Ned Sharp* (Arthur Kennedy); *California Joe* (Charley Grapewin); *Samuel Bacon* (Gene Lockhart); *Crazy Horse* (Anthony Quinn); *Major Romulus Taipe* (Stanley Ridges); *General Philip Sheridan* (John Litel); *William Sharp* (Walter Hampden); *General Winfield Scott* (Sydney Greenstreet); *Fitzhugh Lee* (Regis Toomey); *Callie* (Hattie McDaniel); *Lieutenant Butler* (George P. Huntley, Jr.); *Captain Webb* (Frank Wilcox); *Sergeant Doolittel* (Joseph Sawyer); *Senator Smith* (Minor Watson); *President Grant* (Joseph Crehan); *Salesman* (Irving Bacon); *Captain McCook* (Selmer Jackson); *Corporal Smith* (Eddie Acuff); *Captain Riley* (George Eldridge).

While *The Adventures of Robin Hood* presents Errol Flynn and Olivia de Havilland at their romantic peak as a team, their finest performances together are contained in their eighth and final film, *They Died With Their Boots On.* It is the only one of their pictures in which they are wedded during the course of the story and in which they are seen as a married couple. Since they play an ideally mated pair, it almost seems like a fantasy idealization of the marriage their fans might assume Flynn and Olivia would have had in real life. The fact that *Boots* is an action-packed, adventure epic tends to take away from its being an impressive account of the truly successful marriage of George Armstrong Custer and Elizabeth Bacon. The film is full of historical inaccuracies but it hews to the truth in setting up Elizabeth as a powerful force in Custer's life. It remains for another film to show what a force she was after he died. Custer was only thirty-seven when he went to his death fighting Indians on June 25th, 1876; Libby, as she was called, died in 1933 at the age of ninety and in the 57 years between their deaths, she created and nurtured the image of her husband as a hero. She wrote several books about him, paid for a lauda-

With Errol Flynn and Charley Grapewin

tory biography and lectured. Libby was so liked that no one cared to refute her accounts or doubt her love for the man she idolized. She most certainly would have enjoyed *They Died With Their Boots On*.

Flynn was a good choice for Custer. Both the actor and the soldier were handsome, cavalier figures and laws unto themselves. Lack of self-discipline undermined both their lives. Custer was not the paragon depicted in *Boots* but at the other extreme, neither was he the hysterical, cowardly idiot displayed in *Little Big Man* (1970). His brief career was marked by great personal bravery and quite some brilliance as a cavalry commander, but he was also selfish, ambitious and vainglorious. He was not, as *Boots* suggests, an admirer of the Indians or concerned about their cause. Custer died because he disobeyed orders—he was under the command of General Terry and had been told not to make any moves of his own volition—and he hoped to achieve a personal victory that would win him public approval in his need to clear himself of corruption charges. He was under suspended court martial at the time of his death because of his possible involvement in dispossessing the Indians of their lands in the Dakotas in order to discover gold deposits, which is the opposite of the stance taken by this movie. But for all that, *Boots* presents a good characterization of Custer.

With Errol Flynn

Custer was not quite as poor a West Point cadet as the film almost comically paints him to be. He was commissioned in 1861 ahead of time in order to meet the Union Army's need for officers after the outbreak of the Civil War, a fact which the picture makes clear. It is while on sentry duty that he first meets Libby, the visiting daughter of a pompous judge (Gene Lockhart) from Monroe, Michigan, which is Custer's home town. She asks directions from him and is offended when he fails to speak or stop his pacing. When relieved of guard duty he explains to her that regulations forbid a guard to speak or halt. They laugh about her having trailed him as he walked up and down and Custer, instantly in love, tells her that walking through life with her will be a very pleasant thing. She acts astonished by his boldness but she knows she has met her man. Custer's career in the war is swift and spectacular. By an absurd clerical error—totally unfounded in fact—he is promoted from second lieutenant to brigadier general and is given command of the Michigan Brigade, which he leads to glory. At war's end he is reduced to the rank of captain (factual) and like most officers of that period, he is left without an assignment. Realizing he is desperately unhappy in his inactivity, the socially well-placed Libby goes to see her friend General Winfield Scott (Sydney Greenstreet) and persuades him to find something for her husband. The

With Gene Lockhart and Errol Flynn

fact that she is also a friend of General Philip Sheridan (John Litel), who was the commandant of West Point when Custer was a cadet, is an additional asset.

Custer is promoted to lieutenant-colonel and put in charge of the Seventh Cavalry, stationed at Fort Lincoln in the Dakota Territory. His job is to quell the Indians and help effect colonization, which he does once he whips his regiment into fighting shape. In 1876 he accuses certain business factions of violating Indian treaties and arouses the ire of Ulysses S. Grant, who as a soldier despised Custer and as president considers him dangerous. Custer's accusations cause him to be suspended from his command, but his wife pleads with Sheridan, then commander-in-chief of the army, to reinstate him and allow him to lead his regiment in the Dakota campaign. Custer goes to what he knows will be certain death and leaves Libby with papers that will fix the blame on certain crooked businessmen and politicians. The film ends as Sheridan, at the inquiry, turns to Libby and says, "Come, my dear—your soldier won his final victory." Would that history could be so rewritten.

Despite its cavalier treatment of the facts, *Boots* is a splendidly successful super-western, containing some of the best Civil War footage ever staged, and its depiction of the legendary "Last Stand" is excitingly

brought to life. It was the first time that Raoul Walsh directed a Flynn picture; he took over when the actor finally rebelled against working with stern task-master Michael Curtiz, and while the Curtiz-Flynn swashbucklers are the best of their kind, Walsh found other qualities in Flynn. With Walsh, Flynn projected more of his complex nature, more of the cracks in the heroic plaster. Even though Olivia had no wish to make any more films with him, Flynn insisted on her for the role of Libby. He probably realized that it would be their last film and that he needed her for this depiction of a devoted husband and wife. It cried for an actress who understood him and with whom he could feel at ease—as he seldom did with his female co-stars. "Errol was quite sensitive. I think he knew it would be the last time we would work together." It was a real farewell.

Boots contains what was probably Flynn's best piece of acting and, because of the circumstances, the most poignant. This was Custer's farewell to his wife, which happened to be the last scene Olivia and Flynn ever did. Finely paced by Walsh, with a touching love theme by Max Steiner in the background, Custer prepares to leave as Libby checks all the things he needs. "You know, Libby, they ought to make you the Quartermaster General. Every time I go into the field I'm the best equipped man in the regiment." Both try to maintain a cheerful manner, but then he acciden-

With Hattie McDaniel and Errol Flynn

tally picks up her diary and he reads aloud, "Tomorrow my husband leaves and I cannot help but feel that my last happy days are ended. A premonition of disaster such as I have never known is weighing me down. I try to shut it into my heart but it is almost unbearable. I pray God that I be not asked to walk on alone." Libby tries to laugh it off, "I probably wrote that—or something like it—every time you left . . . you know how foolish women are . . . " Moments later, Custer leaves and says to her, "Walking through life with you, ma'am, has been a very gracious thing." The scene has an almost inevitable air of romantic melancholy about it.

In 1978, at a retrospective showing of some of her films in Los Angeles, Olivia de Havilland found it impossible to sit through the farewell scene of *Boots*. As it began she got up and walked into the lobby, and wept. It is easy to understand why.

With Flynn and director Raoul Walsh

On the set with Flynn during the filming of their final scene

THE MALE ANIMAL

1942
A Warner Bros. Picture,
Produced by Hal B. Wallis,
Directed by Elliott Nugent,
Written by Julius and Philip Epstein and Stephen Morehouse Avery,
    based on the play by James Thurber and Elliott Nugent,
Photographed by Arthur Edeson,
Music by Heinz Roemheld,
101 minutes.

CAST:

Tommy Turner (Henry Fonda); *Ellen Turner* (Olivia de Havilland); *Patricia Stanley* (Joan Leslie); *Joe Ferguson* (Jack Carson); *Ed Keller* (Eugene Pallette); *Michael Barnes* (Herbert Anderson); *Cleota* (Hattie MacDaniel); *Dr. Damon* (Ivan Simpson); *Wally* (Don DeFore); *Hot Garters Garner* (Jean Ames); *Blanche Lamon* (Minna Phillips); *Myrtle Keller* (Regina Wallace); *Coach Sprague* (Frank Mayo); *Alumnus* (Wiliam Davidson); *Nutsy Miller* (Bobby Barnes).

On the set with Fonda

With Jack Carson

Elliott Nugent played the leading role of associate professor Tommy Turner when the play he wrote with James Thurber, *The Male Animal*, first appeared on Broadway in 1940. When Warners turned it into a film they did not want him as its star, since his name meant nothing to moviegoers, but they hired him as its director and gave him his choice of well-known movie actors. Nugent's first choice was Henry Fonda, and Fonda's fine portrayal of the gentle, idealistic teacher is a highlight in his catalogue. Both Nugent and Fonda agreed to Olivia de Havilland as the professor's supportive wife, Ellen. It was not a role that made great demands on her abilities, but her delineation of an intelligent, good-natured woman trying to balance unsettling circumstances in her life is a major contribution to this fine film. *The Male Animal* satirizes the perpetual conflict in American academe—the struggle between the intellectual element and the rah-rah athletic strain. Since it carries the stamp of James Thurber, it also gets in some pertinent comments on the man-woman relationship.

Tommy Turner finds himself with a pair of problems on campus. The first is the appearance of former football star (and eternal undergraduate) Joe Ferguson (Jack Carson), who turns up at his alma mater to whirl the students up with frenzied enthusiasm for the coming Big Game. It also enables him to renew his friendship with Ellen, his schooldays sweetheart. Tommy takes a disliking to the loudmouth, blustering champ, especially when he finds Ellen becoming pleased with his company.

Even more upsetting to Tommy is an editorial written by campus editor Michael Barnes (Herbert Anderson), praising Tommy for his courage to read to his class the last letter written by anarchist Bartolomeo Vanzetti before his execution, a letter expounding the virtues of tolerance. The editorial also berates the school authorities for disregarding liberal-minded teachers like Tommy. Michael happens to be in love with Ellen's sister Pat (Joan Leslie), but she prefers a dashing halfback (Don DeFore). The editorial creates a furor and the dean (Ivan Simpson) warns Tommy that he will likely be dismissed if he reads the letter.

Ellen pleads with Tommy not to read the letter to his students, particularly in view of his possible advancement to a full professorship. Tommy claims the First Amendment is more important than the campus ruckus and makes up his mind to proceed. "You pig-headed fool," she cries, and he counters by making an unfavorable comment on Ferguson, calling him her "paramour." Ellen storms out in anger and goes off to meet Ferguson and some friends, who are having a party. When next Tommy sees her she is downstairs in their living room, dancing with Ferguson. The dejected Tommy says, "Since you two seem so well matched, I'll do the decent thing and step out of your life, Ellen." Again she storms out in anger, and goes with Ferguson to the game. Misery finds company when Tommy and Michael get together and commiserate over drinks. The drunker they get, the more masculine they become. Tommy rants "No tiger would let his mate be stolen. The human animal won't either. I'll fight!"

When Ellen and Joe Ferguson return to the house, the inebriated Tommy challenges the startled former halfback to a fight, but all he succeeds in doing is knocking himself out, after which Ferguson carries him

With Henry Fonda and Jack Carson

With Henry Fonda

With Jack Carson and Don DeFore

upstairs to the bedroom. The situation is beginning to bother the former halfback, since he does not love Ellen and does not want his own life complicated. The next day, almost restored to a semblance of health, Tommy reads the fateful letter to his class. He finds that so many people want to hear the letter that the class has to be given in the auditorium. As he reads the letter, the officers of the school board find that it is touchingly humanistic and contains no political propaganda. Some of them even find themselves shedding tears. The incident makes Tommy a campus hero, and Ellen reaffirms her love for him. Indeed, it was she who slipped the Vanzetti letter into the coat of her absent-minded professor, who would have gone to class without it. The students carry Tommy and Ellen off on a great march around the college, much to the relief of Ferguson. And Pat, too, finds that the intellectual Michael is even more exciting in his fight for freedom of speech than her muscle-bound halfback.

Of all the many movies about college life, *The Male Animal* is one of the few to take sides with the brain factor in favor of the brawn. However, it goes beyond the ribbing of school athletics and takes a few digs at incipient fascism in American academic life. Here the school trustees veer to the Right and seem quite reactionary, particularly the regent, played with flaring nostrils by the bear-like Eugene Pallette. His joy at seeing Ferguson again is both amusing and sinister, as these two mountain-sized Babbitts go into football tackles with childlike relish. Jack Carson is superb as Ferguson, a fatuous football celebrity whose mind and body are both on the verge of turning to blubber. But *The Male Animal* belongs firmly to Fonda, as the quiet man of integrity, part genial dope and part tenacious hanger-on to basic values. Olivia's Ellen is the thoroughly decent, warm-blooded, loving wife with whom every professor should be blest. It is a glowing performance.

With Henry Fonda

IN THIS OUR LIFE

1942
A Warner Bros. Picture,
Produced by Hal B. Wallis,
Directed by John Huston,
Written by Howard Koch, based on the novel by Ellen Glasgow,
Photographed by Ernest Haller,
Music by Max Steiner,
97 minutes.

CAST:

Stanley Timberlake (Bette Davis); *Roy Timberlake* (Olivia de Havilland); *Craig Fleming* (George Brent); *Peter Kingsmill* (Dennis Morgan); *William Fitzroy* (Charles Coburn); *Asa Timberlake* (Frank Craven); *Lavinia Timberlake* (Billie Burke); *Minerva Clay* (Hattie McDaniel); *Betty Wilmoth* (Lee Patrick); *Charlotte Fitzroy* (Mary Servoss); *Parry Clay* (Ernest Anderson); *Jim Purdy* (Willian Davidson); *Dr. Buchanan* (Edward Fielding); *Inspector* (John Hamilton); *Ranger* (William Forrest).

With player, Bette Davis, and John Hamilton

In This Our Life is a Bette Davis picture, made in her prime, which means that anyone else who appeared in it could only be considered secondary. Fortunately, she and Olivia de Havilland had become close friends by this time, and having to take second billing was less irksome to Olivia than it might have been, due to her admiration for Bette and her willingness to work with her. Here the two actresses are sisters—one good and one bad, with not the least doubt in casting as to which would play which. As with so many Davis films of this period, it is the music score by Max Steiner which charges and colors the characterizations and the ambience of the material. Ellen Glasgow's Pulitzer Prize-winning novel about a Virginia family who have lost much of their wealth and position is set up by Steiner in his title music with beautifully descending string cadences that convey an atmosphere of disillusionment. But the real artfulness of the score is in his delineation of the sisters, both with boy's names—Stanley (Bette) and Roy Timberlake (Olivia). The girls are totally different in character and personality. Stanley is spoiled and selfish, and Roy is warm and loving. Stanley is petulant and destructive, and Steiner characterizes her with a fragmentary theme based on a two-note motif, which communicates her neurosis and the lack of resolution in her life. The theme for Roy, on the other hand, is graceful and melodic, and suggests a well-adjusted, nice lady.

The Timberlake family is dominated by the sick, bedridden mother,

With Bette Davis

Lavinia (Billie Burke), who encourages Stanley to take what she can get from life. Lavinia looks upon her husband, Asa (Frank Craven), as soft and ineffectual, while constantly referring to her bachelor brother, William (Charles Coburn), as a paragon of what a man should be. William is wealthy and ruthless in business but he has a failing about which Lavinia knows nothing—a lecherous interest in Stanley, who shrewdly uses him whenever she needs support. In the week before she is to marry lawyer Craig Fleming (George Brent), Stanley takes off with Roy's doctor husband Peter (Dennis Morgan). The distraught Roy agrees to divorce Peter so that he can marry Stanley, but it is not long afterwards that Peter, realizing his folly, commits suicide. In the meantime, Roy and Craig find comfort in each other's company.

When she returns to the Timberlake home, the wily Stanley manages to insinuate herself back into the affections of her family and receive the understanding of Roy. But she is soon up to her old tricks and starts to make a play for Craig, who shows no interest in responding. He refuses to keep a date with Stanley at a roadhouse, and, after waiting in vain, she drives away in fury. It is in this angry state that she hits a woman and a child with her car and fails to stop. The child dies and witnesses identify Stanley's car. She claims that she did not go out that evening and that she had given the car to Parry (Ernest Anderson), the son of the Timberlake cook (Hattie McDaniel) in order that he might wash it. Parry is arrested but his mother swears that he was with her at the time. Roy believes her and asks Craig to handle the case. Stanley refuses to make a confession, even though she is obviously guilty, and in her anguish she turns to Uncle William for solace. To her shock, he finds no interest in her troubles. William has his own troubles; his doctor has told him he has only a short

With George Brent, Frank Craven, Billie Burke, and Bette Davis

With Hattie McDaniel

With Dennis Morgan

194

time to live and he selfishly pleads with Stanley to live with him until the end. Disgusted with the idea and bitter that he can no longer be of help to her, Stanley again drives off at high speed. This time she is spotted by a police car and is pursued when she refuses to stop. Stanley loses control of her car, crashes, and dies.

In the opinion of Bette Davis, *In This Our Life* was a failure to do justice to the novel on which it was based. In fact, she apologized to authoress Glasgow for cheapening her material. Her performance as Stanley Timberlake borders on self-parody as she flounces and indulges in twitches and gestures. No one is more aware of this than Bette herself, who regards it as one of her most overwrought performances. For Olivia the film was relatively easy, since it required a calm, warm portrayal of a very generous-hearted woman. It is only in one scene, where she somewhat bitterly claims that it is time for her to take a leaf out of her sister's book and get some fun out of life that the characterization rings false. It isn't the real Roy Timberlake—or Olivia—speaking. Neither lady could be that glib.

In This Our Life was John Huston's second film as a director, following the success of his *The Maltese Falcon,* and as a gag the cast of his first movie agreed to appear as extras in his second. In the roadhouse sequence, Walter Huston is clearly in evidence as the bartender, but the likes of Humphrey Bogart, Mary Astor, Peter Lorre, and Sydney Greenstreet are barely visible as customers. It was also during the making of this picture that Olivia and John Huston began dating, leading to a lifelong friendship, and other members of the cast were heard to complain that the director was favoring Olivia with flattering camera angles.

With director John Huston and Bette Davis

With George Tobias and Ida
Lupino

THANK YOUR LUCKY STARS

1943
A Warner Bros. First National Picture,
Produced by Mark Hellinger,
Directed by David Butler,
Written by Norman Panama, Melvin Frank, and James V. Kern,
  based on a story by Everett Freeman and Arthur Schwartz,
Photographed by Arthur Edeson,
Songs by Arthur Schwartz and Frank Loesser,
Music direction by Ray Heindorf,
127 minutes:

CAST:

As themselves: Humphrey Bogart, Bette Davis, Olivia de Havilland, Errol Flynn, John Garfield, Ida Lupino, Ann Sheridan, Dinah Shore, Alexis Smith, Jack Carson, Alan Hale, George Tobias, and Eddie Cantor (also in the role of Joe Simpson).

Pat Dixon (Joan Leslie); *Tommy Randolph* (Dennis Morgan); *Farnsworth* (Edward Everett Horton); *Dr. Schlenna* (S. Z. Sakall); *Gossip* (Hattie McDaniel); *Nurse Hamilton* (Ruth Donnelly); *Announcer* (Don Wilson); *Soldier* (Willie Best); *Angelo* (Henry Armetta); *Barney Jackson* (Richard Lane); *Dr. Kirby* (Paul Harvey); *Interne* (James Burke); *Patient* (Bert Gordon); *Olaf* (Mike Mazurki); *Girl with book* (Joyce Reynolds); and Spike Jones and his City Slickers.

Of the several all-star, morale-boosting movies produced during the years of the Second World War, *Thank Your Lucky Stars* is arguably the best. It presents most of the Warner Bros. stars of those vintage years and a generous score of songs by composer Arthur Schwartz and lyricist Frank Loesser. The bill of fare:

The title song, sung by Dinah Shore,
  "Blues in the Night," the Harold Arlen–Johnny Mercer song
    done in mock dramatic fashion by John Garfield,
  "Hotcha Cornia" by Spike Jones and his City Slickers,
  "Ridin' for a Fall," sung by Dennis Morgan and Joan Leslie,
  "We're Staying Home Tonight," sung by Eddie Cantor,
  "Goin' North," sung by Jack Carson and Alan Hale,
  "Love Isn't Born, It's Made," sung by Ann Sheridan, with
    verse spoken by Joyce Reynolds,
  "No You, No Me," sung by Dennis Morgan and Joan Leslie,
  "The Dreamer," sung by Dinah Shore,

"Ice Cold Katie," sung by Hattie McDaniel, Willie Best, Jesse Lee Brooks, Rita Christina, and Chorus,

"How Sweet You are," sung by Dinah Shore,

"That's What You Jolly Well Get," sung by Errol Flynn and Chorus,

"They're Either Too Young or Too Old," sung by Bette Davis,

"The Dreamer," sung by Olivia de Havilland, Ida Lupino, and George Tobias,

"Good Night, Good Neighbor," sung by Dennis Morgan and Chorus,

"Finale," by the entire cast.

The film's plot centers around the staging of a gala benefit show and the frantic efforts of its producers (Edward Everett Horton and S. Z. Sakall) to get it all together. The sub-plot concerns a singer (Dennis Morgan) and a would-be song writer (Joan Leslie) falling in love while trying to break into the movies. The songs are mainly of the "special material" category, with only "They're Either Too Young or Too Old," memorably croaked by Bette Davis, becoming an enduring hit. Errol Flynn, as a boastful Cockney sailor, lampoons his own heroic image, Ann Sheridan gives a knowing musical lecture on the subject of love, and Jack Carson and Alan Hale shine in a spirited vaudeville routine. All in all, a marvelous kind of "amateur night" with the stars.

Olivia de Havilland's appearance in *Thank Your Lucky Stars* is not one of its highlights. She, Ida Lupino, and George Tobias appear in a boogie-woogie version of "The Dreamer," crooned earlier in the picture. Running a scant two minutes and twenty seconds, the three performers belt out the lyrics in raucous fashion, which is amusing only because it is completely at odds with their images. Tobias and Lupino did their own singing but Olivia was dubbed by Lynn Martin. She chews gum throughout the performance—not simply because it helped her "floozie" image in the number but because she found it hard to lip sync to the playback and the chewing made it impossible for the audience to tell whether or not she was mouthing the words properly.

PRINCESS O'ROURKE

1943
A Warner Bros. Picture,
Produced by Hal B. Wallis,
Directed and written by Norman Krasna,
Photographed by Ernest Haller,
Music by Frederick Hollander,
94 minutes.

CAST:

Maria (Olivia de Havilland); *Eddie O'Rourke* (Robert Cummings); *Dave* (Jack Carson); *Jean* (Jane Wyman); *Uncle* (Charles Coburn); *Miss Haskell* (Gladys Cooper); *Supreme Court Justice* (Harry Davenport); *Washburn* (Minor Watson); *G Man* (Ray Walker); *Mrs. Mulvaney* (Nana Bryant); *Mrs. Bowers* (Nydia Westman); *Count* (Curt Bois).

Of the films made toward the end of her Warner period, *Princess O'Rourke* is one of the few for which Olivia de Havilland has genuine regard. For reasons known only to himself, Jack Warner still thought of her as an ingenue and refused to give her roles as women of any real substance or seriousness. Olivia would have loved to have done Bette Davis's role in *The Letter,* and even Davis's part in the trenchant comedy *The Man Who Came to Dinner.* She also asked Warner to let her have the role that went to Ida Lupino in the harsh drama *The Hard Way.* But it seemed as long as Davis and Lupino were in favor, de Havilland would have to settle for the lighter material. *Princess O'Rourke* is light but it is also witty and pointed, with a script by Norman Krasna that won him an Oscar. Since Krasna was also the director, he was able to steer and pace his material precisely as he wished.

Princess Maria (Olivia) is the heir apparent to a European crown, who has been brought to Washington by her diplomat uncle (Charles Coburn) so that he may find an American husband for her. Uncle's opinion of the available European aristocracy is a very low one. As he sees it, the blood lines of the royal eligibles are pretty well played out and what Maria needs is a robust Yankee to give her some healthy children. Feeling exhausted by all the efforts made by her uncle, Maria decides to take a vacation on a dude ranch out west and gets on a plane piloted by Eddie O'Rourke (Robert Cummings). To calm her nerves, Maria takes some sleeping pills, which prove to be stronger than she had imagined, with the result that she cannot wake up when O'Rourke lands his plane. Not knowing what else to do with her, he takes her to his apartment so that she can sleep off her pills. In this action he is abetted by his co-pilot, Dave (Jack Carson), and Dave's bride-to-be Jean (Jane Wyman). By the end of their first day together, neither Maria nor Eddie can face the idea of not being together. He proposes, she accepts, and they go back to Washington to break the news to uncle, who is aghast. He wanted her to marry an American, but one of some wealth and station, not a mere pilot.

Maria insists on marrying the man of her choice, and uncle finally agrees when he learns that Eddie comes from a line of prolific forbears, noted for the preponderance of sons they produced. Since uncle is a guest of Franklin Delano Roosevelt at the White House, he is able to arrange for the wedding in one of its rooms, with a Supreme Court justice (Harry Davenport) doing the honors. As the prenuptial arrangements are being made, Eddie suddenly has a change of heart—not about Maria but at the idea of suddenly becoming a morganatic nonentity and no longer a citizen of the United States. His patriotic outburst upsets uncle and disturbs Maria. She gives the matter a little thought and arrives at the conclusion that Eddie is more important to her than her royal standing. She becomes Mrs. O'Rourke, ex-princess. A surreptitious marriage is arranged at night in the White House, with FDR—by inference— hovering outside the door and nodding approval.

Princess O'Rourke is a kind of Cinderella-in-reverse tale and quite a lot like the Audrey Hepburn picture *Roman holiday* (1953). Permission was received from the White House for a limited use of the premises and President Roosevelt liked the idea of his presence being utilized in the picture. He even allowed his dog Falla to play in a scene, in which the little Scottie carries a note between the lovers. The film did well at the box office and it was on the preliminary listing at the Motion Picture Academy for Best Film of 1943. Although it did not make the final list, *Princess O'Rourke* found a very warm reception at the White House. Aside from its somewhat overstressed patriotism, the film stills plays amusingly, thanks to Krasna's excellent script. For Olivia it was a pleasing and satisfying assignment, balancing the dignity of a princess with the glow of a young lady in love.

With Robert Cummings and Jack Carson

With Minor Watson, Robert Cummings and Charles Coburn

*With Jack Carson, Jane
Wyman, Robert Cummings,
Charles Coburn and Minor
Watson*

With Charles Coburn

GOVERNMENT GIRL

1943
An RKO Picture,
Produced and directed by Dudley Nichols,
Written by Dudley Nichols, based on a story by Adela Rogers St. John,
Photographed by Frank Redman,
Music by Leigh Harline,
94 minutes.

CAST:

Smokey (Olivia de Havilland); *Browne* (Sonny Tufts); *May* (Anne Shirley); *Dana* (Jess Barker); *Sergeant Joe* (James Dunn); *Branch* (Paul Stewart); *Mrs. Wright* (Agnes Moorehead); *Senator McVickers* (Harry Davenport); *Mrs. Harris* (Una O'Connor); *Ambassador* (Sig Rumann); *Miss Trask* (Jane Darwell); *Count Bodinsky* (George Givot); *Mrs. Harvester* (Paul Stanton); *Marqueenie* (Art Smith); *Miss McVickers* (Joan Valerie); *Mr. Gibson* (Harry Shannon); *Tom Halliday* (Ray Walker); *The Chief* (Emory Parnell).

With Sonny Tufts

A week after finishing her work on *Princess O'Rourke*, Olivia de Havilland was loaned to RKO, at the behest of Dudley Nichols, who felt she was just right to play the title role in his *Government Girl*. Nichols had long been a distinguished screen writer, with successes such as *The Informer, The Hurricane, Bringing Up Baby*, and *Stagecoach*, but now he wanted to become his own boss. *Government Girl* was Nichols' debut as a director-producer, but it would not be a picture that he or Olivia would find beneficial to their careers. Seen today it is a mildly amusing reminder of the chaos of wartime Washington, with its morass of bureaucracy, its shortage of manpower, its abundance of women, and particularly its lack of sufficient accomodation, all of which was dealt with much more stylishly by Columbia in *The More the Merrier*, released a half-year before.

Smokey Allard (Olivia) is a spirited government secretary and because she knows a lot about the ways and means of Washington, she is assigned to an industrialist (Sonny Tufts) when the government puts him in charge of bomber production with instructions to double previous output. Known for his efficiency and used to the ways of private industry, he does as ordered, but steps on important toes to do it and reveals a disdain for red tape. The sacred rule of Capitol Hill mean little to him, so little that he eventually ends up having to defend himself before a Senate committee. He is acquitted, mostly due to the efforts of the trusty Smokey, who reminds the committee of his success and points out that he

is free of any actual breaking of the law. The impetuous industrialist may have shattered a few precedents, but this is war! Besides, she loves him.

Government Girl began production in August of 1943 and was in the theatres by November. Perhaps Nichols was trying to emulate the industrialist of his script and show Hollywood bureaucracy a thing or two about turning out pictures, but the film shows signs of being produced too fast, with some rough editing and uneven pacing. Nonetheless, it did well enough to make a profit and proved that Nichols was capable of more than simply writing screenplays. He did well as a writer-director-producer with *Sister Kenny* in 1946, but with the failure of *Mourning Becomes Electra* the following year, Nichols decided to return to writing.

Government Girl has some nice moments. Anne Shirley is good as another government girl, sharing a hotel suite with Smokey and desperate to get it for herself and her soldier groom (James Dunn), and Jess Barker is effective as the handsome young bureaucrat who loves Smokey and tries to create trouble for the industrialist. Sonny Tufts plays the latter with the genial oafishness on which he seemed to have held a patent. As for Olivia, it was a light romp, requiring her to be pert and lively, and even to whiz around Washington on a little motor bike. Not a bad role, but still a long way from the really good material for which she craved.

With Anne Shirley and Una O'Connor

THE WELL-GROOMED BRIDE

1946
A Paramount Picture,
Produced by Fred Kohlmar,
Directed by Sidney Lanfield,
Written by Claude Binyon and Robert Russell,
Photographed by John F. Seitz,
Music by Roy Webb,
75 minutes.

CAST:

Margie (Olivia de Havilland); *Lt. Briggs* (Ray Milland); *Torchy* (Sonny Tufts); *Capt. Hornby* (James Gleason); *Rita Sloane* (Constance Dowling); *Mr. Dawson* (Percy Kilbride); *Wickley* (Jean Heather); *Mitch* (Jay Norris); *Buck* (Jack Reilly); *Goose* (George Turner); *Justice* (Tom Fadden); *Hotel Clerk* (Donald Beddoe); *Major Smith* (William Forrest).

The Well-Groomed Bride was far from a well-groomed return to the screen for Olivia de Havilland after an absence of almost three years. By rights it should have been only two years but Paramount did not release this limp comedy until January of 1946, though it had been completed the previous spring. Not that Olivia cared very much. She had accepted a Paramount offer for two films and decided to do *The Well-Groomed Bride* when Paulette Goddard could not go ahead with it due to pregnancy. Olivia was still awaiting the Supreme Court of California's decision on her legal clearance from Warner Bros. and she was impressed with the fact that Paramount was willing to go ahead with the film even though the decision had not been handed down yet. No sooner did she start work than she learned that the ruling was in her favor and that she was finally clear of Warners. Had the decision been made a week earlier, she doubtless would not have become involved in *The Well-Groomed Bride,* and would have waited for something better.

Here Olivia is Margie Dawson in San Francisco in the final year of the Second World War, welcoming home her army lieutenant fiance Torchy (Sonny Tufts) after he has been stationed for two years in the Aleutian Islands. To celebrate she has somehow acquired the only magnum of French champagne in town, a fact which comes to the attention of naval lieutenant Dudley Briggs (Ray Milland). He has been instructed by his commandng officer, Captain Hornby (James Gleason), to get a magnum of French champagne at any cost in order to christen an aircraft carrier,

With Ray Milland and William Edmonds

which is being named in honor of France. Dudley pleads with Margie to no avail. He does everything he can to get it, including trying to steal it. He spends so much time with Margie that he starts to fall in love with the pretty but firm-minded young lady. Her problems are worsened by the antics of her fiance, who is a former football star and very conceited. He is constantly being dragged off to appear here and there to please his admirers, and Margie begins to wonder what kind of a life she will have sharing him with the public. The rivalry between the army and the navy does little to bring sanity to her dizzy predicament. The solution comes when Margie decides that Dudley is the man for her and not Torchy, and at the ship's christening it is Margie who does the honors and Torchy who hands over the magnum for the occasion.

A rather strained comedy, with its three stars working overtime to give it some fizz, the best that can be said about this picture is that it brought Olivia back to the screen.

With Constance Dowling and Sonny Tufts

With Ray Milland and Sonny Tufts

DEVOTION

1944
A Warner Bros. Picture,
Produced by Robert Buckner,
Directed by Curtis Bernhardt,
Written by Keith Winter, based on a story by Theodore Reeves,
Photographed by Ernest Haller,
Music by Erich Wolfgang Korngold,
107 minutes.

CAST:

Charlotte Brontë (Olivia de Havilland); *Emily Brontë* (Ida Lupino); *Ann Brontë* (Nancy Coleman); *Arthur Nichols* (Paul Henreid); *Thackeray* (Sydney Greenstreet); *Branwell Brontë* (Arthur Kennedy); *Lady Thornton* (Dame May Whitty); *Monsieur Heger* (Victor Francen); *Reverend Brontë* (Montagu Love); *Aunt Branwell* (Ethel Griffies); *Madame Heger* (Odette Myrtil); *Sir John Thornton* (Edmond Breon); *Tabby* (Marie de Becker); *Butcher* (Donald Stuart); *Hoggs* (Forrester Harvey).

Olivia de Havilland's final film under her Warner Bros. contract was *Devotion*, the story of the Bronte family, which had been planned for years and which the studio believed would be in the same league with their successful biographies about Emile Zola, Louis Pasteur, Paul Ehrlich, Mark Twain, *et al.* At one point there were plans to have Bette Davis play Charlotte Brontë, with Miriam Hopkins as sister Emily. By the time the picture went into production, Olivia had been cast as Charlotte, Ida Lupino as Emily, Nancy Coleman as Anne, the youngest sister, and Arthur Kennedy as brother Branwell, with the film's title presumably denoting their familial loyalty. The result was a handsome, romantic picture, with fine sets and costumes, a rapturous score by Erich Korngold, and some of the gothic ambience that marks the Goldwyn version of *Wuthering Heights* (1939) and the Joan Fontaine–Orson Welles account of *Jane Eyre* (1944). However, as a realistic telling of the Brontë story, *Devotion* is preposterously glossy and fanciful. American literary scholars were disdainful of it; British scholars were downright furious. The film communicates little of the harshness of life on the Yorkshire moors in the early nineteenth century, none of its severe weather, and only a suggestion of the meagre lifestyle of the Brontës. All three actresses are too robust, and certainly too well dressed. In actual fact, Charlotte died in 1855 at the age of thirty-nine; Emily was thirty; and Anne lived to be only twenty-four. The alcoholic Branwell also died in his twenties. *Devotion* looks rather as if the sce-

With Ida Lupino, Arthur Kennedy, and Paul Henreid

narists had just finished reading *Little Women.*

The film opens in the village of Haworth in 1836, as Lady Thornton (Dame May Whitty) donates wrapping paper to the Brontë girls, since they cannot afford to buy writing paper for their prodigious output of poems, essays, and stories. The girls, and Branwell, live with their widowed father, the local vicar (Montagu Love) and their Aunt Branwell (Ethel Griffies). Branwell is an artist, always sneering at his sisters and frequently drunk. Most of his income is picked up in public houses, sketching the patrons. One evening he is helped home by the newly arrived curate, Arthur Nichols (Paul Henreid), whom the girls assume to be a fellow drunk. They are busy with preparations to become governesses in order to finance Branwell's trip to London to establish himself as a painter.

With Paul Henreid and Ida Lupino

Branwell soon returns from London, bitter at being a misunderstood genius. Emily comes to know and appreciate Nichols, whom she helps out in Sunday school. She takes him to the moors and shows him a craggy plateau she loves. It is strange, grey, and stormswept. She tells him it is the place she writes about and that it is inhabited by ghosts, "I call it Wuthering Heights." She also tells Nichols about an imagined rider on a great, black horse, who seems to beckon to her.

With Ida Lupino and Victor Francen

Charlotte, pretty, ambitious, and charmingly arrogant, treats Nichols with veiled contempt and tells him not to see her sister again. He responds by kissing Charlotte. Later he buys one of Branwell's paintings, in order to provide money for the education of Charlotte and Emily in Brussels. Emily visits Nichols in his quarters and confesses her love for him, but he tells her he cannot respond in kind. In Brussels, the two girls are amazed at the amorous advances of the suave headmaster, Henri Heger (Victor Francen), and Charlotte allows herself to have a crush on him. She imagines she is learning something about "life." They leave the school and return to Yorkshire when they hear that Branwell is seriously ill, a sad fact somewhat lightened by the publication of some of their poems. Branwell, having read the manuscripts of Charlotte's *Jane Eyre* and Emily's *Wuthering Heights,* points out to his sisters that they are in love with the same man. Shortly thereafter, Branwell dies. The two novels are published with great success in London.

The feisty Charlotte goes to London to enjoy her success, but Emily, ever brooding and increasingly ill, prefers to stay home. In London, Charlotte is befriended by the elegant, imperious author William Makepeace Thackeray (Sydney Greenstreet), who takes her to fashionable restaurants and for rides in Hyde Park. She is delighted with the attention. She asks him, "Do they always stare at you in public?" He smiles, "They're staring at you, my dear." She tells him, "My brother Branwell always said that to ride in the park with Thackeray was the height of success." His response is immediate, "He was quite right, of course. It is!" Then, in talking about Emily, from whom she feels somewhat estranged, Charlotte says, "Emily has never experienced a great romantic passion." Thackeray raises a knowing eyebrow. "When was the last time you read *Wuthering Heights?*" he asks.

A little later Thackeray drives Charlotte to see Arthur Nichols, who is now assigned to Limehouse. Nichols admits he loves her, but they quarrel and she returns to Haworth, where Emily is now desperately ill. Not long after, Emily dies, sitting in a chair looking out of a window as her imaginary horseman rides toward her and envelopes her in his huge black cloak. Charlotte now understands her sister's quiet integrity and her unrequited love. Nichols returns to Yorkshire, and together they pay their respects to the memory of Emily on Wuthering Heights.

Devotion is a picturization of legend, taking a rather cavalier attitude toward the facts, not the least being that Emily died before Charlotte was celebrated in London as the authoress of *Jane Eyre*. Legend has it that the two sisters loved the same man, but the film implies that the inspiration for Charlotte's Edward Rochester and Emily's Heathcliff was Arthur Nichols, played in a mild manner by Paul Henreid. It is more likely that the inspiration for both of those troubled characters was brother Branwell, played floridly by Arthur Kennedy. Ida Lupino is fine as the wan Emily, and Olivia revels in the grand manners of Charlotte, although the part is ill defined as written and directed. *Devotion* is not a bad film as a piece of entertainment. What it needs is the same attitude one takes toward *The Charge of the Light Brigade*—a total suspension of any knowledge of history.

Rehearsing with Sydney Greenstreet

TO EACH HIS OWN

With John Lund

1946
A Paramount Picture,
Produced by Charles Brackett,
Directed by Mitchell Leisen,
Written by Charles Brackett and Jacques Thery,
Photographed by Daniel L. Fapp,
Music by Victor Young,
122 minutes.

CAST:

Josephine Norris (Olivia de Havilland); *Bart Cosgrove/Gregory Piersen* (John Lund); *Corinne Piersen* (Mary Anderson); *Lord Desham* (Roland Culver); *Alex Piersen* (Phillip Terry); *Mac Tilton* (Bill Goodwin); *Liz Lorrimer* (Virginia Welles); *Daisy Gingras* (Victoria Horne); *Mr. Norris* (Griff Barnett); *Belle Ingram* (Alma Macrorie); *Griggsy at age five* (Bill Ward); *Babe* (Frank Faylen); *Dr. Hunt* (Willard Robertson); *Mr. Clinton* (Arthur Loft); *Mrs. Clinton* (Virginia Farmer); *Miss Pringle* (Doris Lloyd); *Mr. Harkett* (Clyde Cook); *Miss Claflin* (Ida Moore); *Mrs. Rix* (Mary Young).

With Bill Ward

"When Paramount sent me the script of *To Each His Own*, I knew immediately it was a part I had to do. It was a very long part and it offered a lot of opportunities for an actress; it was fascinating to see how the character changed. Yet I knew it would be difficult to make a sentimental story such as this believable." Olivia de Havilland's instincts as an actress were keen indeed in regard to this greatly successful movie. The role offered even more than she anticipated, and the end result was her first Oscar, and she was right in assuming the difficulties of bringing the material to the screen with conviction. The story of an unwed mother giving up her baby and yearning to have him back was not a sure-fire attraction for 1946 audiences. It was more in line with the soap operas of the Thirties, such as *Madame X, Stella Dallas,* and *The Old Maid.* No one was more aware of this than Mitchell Leisen, who refused to take on the job of direction when producer-writer Charles Brackett approached him with the project. It was Olivia who finally persuaded Leisen to do it. She reasoned that it needed his kind of finesse, his eye for detail, his firm hand in controlling sentiment, and his empathy for actors. With Olivia refusing to do the film with any other director, Paramount managed to bring Leisen into an agreement, which included giving him command of all pre-production work on the film and script approval. The gentlemanly Leisen began directing with his customary skill, but he still had some reservations about the story. However, by the end of the first week his enthusiasm was as high as that of his star.

To Each His Own uses the time-honored device of the flashback to set up its story, but like everything else in this meticulously made picture, it is done with stylish effectiveness. The film starts in the last year of the Second World War in London as a middle-aged American businesswoman named Josephine Norris (Olivia) confides in Lord Desham (Roland Culver) as they perform their air-raid-observer duties. Josephine has heard that an airman, Gregory Pierson (John Lund), is about to arrive in London and she is nervously anxious to meet him. She has not seen him since he was a boy, and the reason for her anxiety is that he is her son, a fact of which he is unaware.

In 1917, Josephine, known to all as Jody, is a lovely, innocent small-town girl who falls in love with a young aviator (also Lund). After a while he admits that his first intention was merely to seduce her but her sweet nature quickly leads him to a more sincere regard and a proposal of marriage. A while later Jody learns that the aviator has been killed in action, a blow that is made the more severe by her pregnancy. Jody leaves town in order to have her baby boy and thereafter allows him to be adopted by her friend Corinne Pearson (Mary Anderson), a decision she almost immediately regrets. A few years later, now a prosperous executive in the cosmetics business, Jody ruthlessly manages to get custody of little Gregory and showers him with generosity. But it is all in vain, because all Gregory wants to do is get back to his "real" mother. Realizing her scheme has failed, Jody sends the boy back to Corinne and then moves to London to live.

Jody evolves into the more austerely named Josephine Norris, a rather prim but shrewd lady who has decided to devote herself to the business world and avoid men and marriage. When he arrives in London in 1944, Gregory calls on Jody on the advice of his "real mother" and Jody invites him to stay at her apartment in London. He is grateful but otherwise oblivious of her. His thoughts are centered on the lovely English girl (Virginia Welles) he plans to marry. While Josephine has no intention of revealing her identity, she hopes to have her son around for the mere pleasure of being able to help him. She laments to Lord Desham, "I'd like to give him the sun and the moon and the stars. All his life I've wanted to. I hoped this week I could feel like a real mother—showering things on him, spoiling him. All he wants is his girl. I can't help him there." Lord Desham, on the other hand, does help. Not only does he facilitate the wedding but he drops enough gradual clues for Gregory to realize just who this generous lady is. At the wedding reception it all finally dawns on him. He walks up to Josephine Norris and says, "I think this is our dance, Mother."

It is no snide comment to call *To Each His Own* a "woman's picture." It

is all of that, in the best possible ways, with a sincere probing of the female psyche and problems common to women. The scripting is precise and the balance between sentiment and reality is a tribute to Mitchell Leisen's taste, a fact clearly heralded by Olivia: "Mitch was a marvelous director from an actor's point of view. We would talk over the emotions of the scene, the characters, and what they were thinking. But it was always Mitch who knew how to take all the raw material and make the film. Whenever I needed help, he knew what to tell me. Then I could see it, then I could do it."

The character of Josephine Norris is the whole body of the film and it was skillfully crafted by writer Brackett and his director. She emerges from a sweet girl into a somewhat hardened young woman into a wisely contented middle-aged matron. To help delineate the periods of the story, Olivia used various perfumes for each stage of the character's growth, with the inspired Edith Head cunningly designing clothes to reinforce the changes in her personality. Leisen also instructed his camera crew to light Olivia differently at the various points in the story.

Biographer David Chierichetti discussed the role with Mitchell Leisen: "Olivia was so wonderful in that part. Nobody else could have played it as well as she did, to be so beautiful and innocent in the beginning, then grow to be a bitch and finally the lonely Miss Norris. Olivia is a very flexible actress. She listens to what you have to say, and she will do her best to do it as you want it. Olivia and I worked it all out together. She always came up to me before each scene and said, 'Now tell me what I'm thinking.' I gave it to her and she said, 'Now give me my pitch.' She used her normal voice at the beginning and as she grew older, her voice dropped in pitch, lower and lower, until it became the voice of a mature woman."

So convinced was he that Olivia was going to win an Oscar, Leisen gave a party at the end of the film's shooting and handed her a charm bracelet with a tiny miniature Oscar on it. Leisen was, of course, absolutely right in his prediction. Olivia's Academy Award was not merely a prize for a superb piece of film acting, but it was also a justification for the years of fighting with Warner Bros. for better roles, and proof positive that she was indeed capable of all that she believed she could be as an actress.

With John Lund

THE DARK MIRROR

1946
A Universal Picture,
Produced by Nunnally Johnson,
Directed by Robert Siodmak,
Written by Nunnally Johnson, based on the novel by Vladimir Pozner,
Photographed by Milton Krasner,
Music by Dimitri Tiomkin,
85 minutes.

With Thomas Mitchell

CAST:

Terry and Ruth Collins (Olivia de Havilland); *Dr. Scott Elliott* (Lew Ayres); *Lt. Stevenson* (Thomas Mitchell); *Rusty* (Richard Long); *District Attorney Girard* (Charles Evans); *Franklin* (Garry Owens); *George Benson* (Lester Allen); *Mrs. Didrikson* (Lela Bliss); *Miss Beade* (Marta Mitrovich); *Photo-Double* (Amelita Ward); *Sergeant Temple* (William Halligan); *Mrs. O'Brien* (Ida Moore); *Janitor* (Charles McAvoy).

The challenge of playing two roles in a film is one no red-blooded actress can resist, and Olivia de Havilland received her chance with *The Dark Mirror*. It went beyond the mere playing of two roles; here the challenge was difficult in the extreme, since the roles were those of twins who almost defy telling apart and yet one is nice and normal and the other is mad and murderous. Milton Krasner's photography and the special effects of J. Devereaux Jennings and Paul Lerpae allowed Olivia to spend a great deal of time with herself on the screen, to converse at intimate range and to actually touch. Combining psychiatry with crime detection called for a stylish director, and producer-writer Nunnally Johnson made a wise choice in the Hungarian-born Robert Siodmak, who had proved his flair for suspense and darkly mooded mayhem with *The Suspect* (1945), *The Spiral Staircase* (1946), and *The Killers* (1946).

Siodmak's movie starts with his camera prowling around an apartment and finding the dead body of a society doctor. Detective Lieutenant Stevenson (Thomas Mitchell) pins the blame on Ruth Collins, who works at a newsstand in a medical building and who has been seen with the deceased. His case is destroyed by the appearance of sister Ruth and the inability of the witnesses to distinguish one girl from the other. One has a perfect alibi, and they stick together in supporting each other. It then occurs to Stevenson to ask aid from a psychiatrist, Dr. Elliott (Lew Ayres), who specializes in the study of the psychology of twins. He puts the sisters through a series of tests, including the Rorschach ink blots, lie detector,

With Lew Ayres

With Thomas Mitchell, Lew Ayres and Garry Owens

and word assocation. From this he gathers that Ruth is totally sane and Terry isn't, and that she is very likely to kill again. Elliott falls in love with the gentle Ruth and she with him, a circumstance that is made complicated by Terry's also falling in love with him. She now has a reason to try and get rid of her sister, hopefully by persuading her that she is insane and guilty.

It soon becomes apparent to Elliott that Ruth is in danger and that Terry must be tricked into revealing herself. Ruth finds it impossible to believe that her sister could be guilty but she agrees to Elliott's scheme, which is to persuade Terry that Ruth has died. At the girls' apartment, Terry tells Elliott and Stevenson of Ruth's guilt in killing the doctor and how concerned she has been for her declining sanity. As Terry carries on with this line, Ruth walks in from the bedroom to face her demented, treacherous sister. Realizing she has been tricked, Terry breaks into a fit of hatred for Ruth, who finally has to realize that Terry is hopelessly and viciously insane. Her comfort is in knowing she is loved by Elliott.

The Dark Mirror is a tour-de-force for Olivia, who skillfully managed to mark the differences in the seemingly identical twins. The part of Terry is the more difficult, since it required a semblance of normality in order for the girl to convince the other characters that she is sane and to subtly shift suspicion to Ruth. The night scene of the girls in twin beds is especially effective, as the cunning Terry talks to her sleeping sister and tries to implant the idea of insanity. She jolts her awake by flashing a light in her eyes and then comforts her by saying she will always be there to help her. However, the film's most arresting scene is the concluding one, with the tricked Terry lapsing into near savagery. It is an almost frighteningly convincing piece of acting.

The film suffers from some rather glib psychiatric talk about twins being a reflection of one another's good and bad qualities, but Siodmak's sly direction covers up the dubious verbiage and produces a taut, disturbing tale. The really heavy work in the film is, obviously, Olivia's. She claims it was a particularly exacting picture to make: "The technical problems involved in playing a dual role were extremely difficult to solve, and that horrible Terry I had to play in that picture haunts me to this day." That last point is one Olivia has made on many occasions. If one wants to get her to shudder, he has only to mention Terry Collins, the heartless psychopath of *The Dark Mirror*.

THE SNAKE PIT

1946
1948
A 20th Century-Fox Picture,
Produced by Darryl F. Zanuck,
Directed by Anatole Litvak,
Written by Frank Partos and Millen Brand, based on the novel by
   Mary Jane Ward,
Photographed by Leo Tover,
Music by Alfred Newman,
108 minutes.

With Celeste Holme

CAST:

Virginia Cunningham (Olivia de Havilland); *Robert Cunningham* (Mark Stevens); *Dr. Mark Kirk* (Leo Genn); *Grace* (Celeste Holm); *Dr. Terry* (Glenn Langan); *Miss Davis* (Helen Craig); *Gordon* (Leif Erickson); *Mrs. Greer* (Beulah Bondi); *Dr. Curtis* (Howard Freeman); *Mrs. Stuart* (Natalie Schafer); *Ruth* (Ruth Donnelly); *Margaret* (Katharine Locke); *Dr. Gifford* (Frank Conroy); *Miss Hart* (Minna Gombell); *Miss Bixby* (June Storey); *Valerie* (Ann Doran); *Mr. Stuart* (Damian O'Flynn); *Inmates* (Lee Patrick, Isabel Jewell, Victoria Horne, Tamara Shayne, and Grace Poggi).

A pale, sickly young woman named Virginia Cunningham sits on a park bench and hears voices asking her questions. Who is she? How is she? Where is she? She answers politely but wonders to herself why she is being questioned. She is as annoyed as she is puzzled. Virginia has reason to be puzzled; she is a patient in a state institution for the mentally ill and unaware of it. All she knows, while trying to remain aloof from the confusion, is that she is constantly being questioned and herded around with masses of other strange women in a huge, busy, dingy building.

With Mark Stevens

This is how *The Snake Pit* begins—and for Olivia de Havilland it is the beginning of the most difficult of all her film roles and the one requiring the most preparation, even to the extent of losing weight and deliberately making herself look gaunt. By contemporary standards, after so many years of filmic violence and searing reality, *The Snake Pit* does not seem a brave picture to make, but in 1948 it was more than a brave venture: It was highly risky as screen entertainment for the masses and the first time the subject of mental illness was treated in an intelligent and extended fashion in Hollywood. The initial credit goes to Anatole Litvak, who put up $75,000 of his own money to buy the rights to Mary Jane Ward's novel before it was published and then tried to get various producers in Hollywood to turn it into a film. After a number of rejections he went to Darryl

F. Zanuck, for whom he had directed *This Above All* in 1942. Zanuck was a little scared of the property but he believed it should be made. Zanuck, more than most Hollywood producers, realized that audiences had changed with the war and that the screen should be bolder in tackling the problems of current life. He had already tackled anti-Semitism in *Gentleman's Agreement* (1947) and he was getting ready to tackle racial prejudice in *Pinky*. After reading Litvak's outline of the screenplay, Zanuck gave his permission to proceed. As with all the films in which he was deeply interested, Zanuck carefully supervised the scripting and the shooting, and later brought his considerable acumen as a film editor to bear in order to intensify Litvak's moods of urgency and suspense. The point Zanuck most wanted to stress was that despite the film's being a revelation of the despair of the mentally ill and the mostly inadequate facilities extended to them, the story had to focus on Virginia Cunningham in order to capture the attention of the audience and make its points.

Virginia has been placed in the institution by her husband (Mark Stevens), not to get rid of her but to arrive at the quickest possible cure and to resume his life with her. He is fortunate that Virginia comes under the care of Dr. Kirk (Leo Genn), a gentle and deeply compassionate man, who manages to find the time, amid the overcrowded chaos, to help Virginia emerge from her state of schizophrenia and extreme feelings of guilt. From the husband he learns that Virginia was a frustrated writer at the time of their meeting and that not long after their marriage she became increasingly depressed and irrational, and finally lapsed into a breakdown. By analysis, supplemented by hydrotherapy and electric shock treatments, Kirk peals back the layers of her condition and finds that she was emotionally distraught as a child, due to a domineering mother and an over-attachment to her father, who died when she was still young. As a young woman she had dated a man (Leif Erickson) and had been with him when he was killed in a car accident. Virginia has therefore grown up with the feeling that she is fatal to men, and after her marriage had thought of herself as a hazard to her loving husband. Dr. Kirk, after much treatment, brings her to the point where she understands and accepts all this and can return to her home.

Virginia's treatment is far from simple and there are times when she seems to regress rather than progress. A lot of this is due to the state of the hospital, more crowded than it should be, and the work burden placed upon doctors and nurses. *The Snake Pit* makes all this chillingly clear. It does not make villains of the hospital personnel but shows them to be humans with their own problems and shortcomings. The title of the story comes from the ancient habit of throwing lunatics into a snake pit in order to shock them into sanity. Litvak dramatizes this horrible attitude in one memorable overhead shot in which he blurs the edges of his screen, focuses on Virginia in the middle of a crowd of whirling, noisy

With Ruth Donnelly

women, and pulls back his camera to achieve the effect of a pit. For the viewer it is almost as electrifying as the shock treatment rendered the patients.

Litvak hired two psychiatrists as his advisers and kept them on the set all through the filming, making them available to the writers and the cast. He spent three months of preparation, observing standards and methods in mental hospitals, and required his principal actors to accompany him on some of the investigative work. Olivia visited the institution at Camarillo, California: "I went three times to do research. It was regarded as a model hospital but it was sadly undermanned as to doctors. There I talked to and watched inmates in varying degrees of mental illness. I steeled myself to look at these cases objectively, the same as I did when I witnessed two births as research for a scene in *Gone With the Wind*."

Olivia was especially pleased to know that authoress Ward had her in mind for the role of Virginia, as did Litvak, and so there was no hesitation on her part in accepting the invitation to do the film. It was full of challenges in the extreme, not the least of which was the physical discomfort the role required. For the hydrotherapy scene Olivia was placed in a tank and had hundreds of gallons of water poured on her. She had to simulate the electric shock therapy and found it almost as upsetting as the real thing. But nothing was more upsetting than witnessing real patients in pitiful states of condition. However, it was from this observation that she and Litvak were able to arrive at the end result, which to Zanuck's relief became not only a critical success but a money maker for 20th Century-Fox.

Olivia places the success of her characterization as Virginia on a chance meeting with a patient at Camarillo. "I met a young woman who was very much like Virginia, about the same age and physical description, as well as being a schizophrenic with guilt problems. She had developed, like Virginia, a warm rapport with her doctor, but what struck me most of all was the fact that she was rather likable and appealing. It hadn't occurred to me before that a mental patient could be appealing, and it was that that gave me the key to the performance."

There was no doubt about Olivia's being nominated for an Academy Award. She lost out to Jane Wyman, for *Johnny Belinda*, but she did receive the prestigious New York Film Critics Circle Award as the Best Actress of 1949. There were a few other awards but the most satisfying was the fact that *The Snake Pit* brought wide public attention to the plight of mental institutions which resulted in a certain amount of change in the laws, and support and administration of them.

With Leo Genn

With Mark Stevens

THE HEIRESS

With Montgomery Clift

1949
A Paramount Picture,
Produced and directed by William Wyler,
Written by Ruth and Augustus Goetz, from their stage play based on
    the novel *Washington Square* by Henry James,
Photographed by Leo Tover,
Music by Aaron Copland,
115 minutes.

CAST:

Catherine Sloper (Olivia de Havilland); *Morris Townsend* (Montgomery Cliff); *Dr. Austin Sloper* (Ralph Richardson); *Lavinia Penniman* (Miriam Hopkins); *Maria* (Vanessa Brown); *Marian Almond* (Mona Freeman); *Jefferson Almond* (Ray Collins); *Mrs. Montgomery* (Betty Linley); *Elizabeth Almond* (Selena Royle); *Arthur Townsend* (Paul Lees); *Mr. Abeel* (Harry Antrim); *Quintus* (Russ Conway); *Geier* (David Thursby).

Olivia de Havilland's second Oscar was the result of her performance as Catherine Sloper in *The Heiress*, a role that bears some relationship to her first Oscar performance inasmuch as both are studies of women who progress from extreme innocence to maturity via painful exposure to life's vicissitudes. *The Heiress*, punctiliously directed by William Wyler, is a film of genuine quality on every level. Oscars also went to composer Aaron Copland, set designers John Meehan and Harry Horner, and costume designers Edith Head and Gile Steele. The film itself was nominated for Best Picture but lost to *All the King's Men*, and it did only moderately well at the box office. *The Heiress* sadly serves to prove that films of great taste and intelligence seldom please the masses. Part of the quality of the film came from the decision to allow Ruth and Augustus Goetz, who had written the stage play based on Henry James's *Washington Square*, to be fully responsible for the screenplay.

Catherine Sloper is a naive, sheltered, and shy young woman who lives with her father, Dr. Austin Sloper (Ralph Richardson), a wealthy resident of New York's Washington Square, circa 1850. Dr. Sloper makes it obvious that he has little regard for his plain daughter, who has none of the beauty or sparkle of her late mother. She strives to please her father, but his coldly condescending manner causes her to be ever more withdrawn and insecure. Her only asset is financial—Catherine has an annual allowance of $10,000 from her mother's estate and as his only child she will receive all of her father's wealth. Despite all this she has been unable to attract and hold the interest of men—that is, until Morris Townsend (Montgomery Clift) comes along. He has dissipated his own funds and sees in Catherine a chance for security. He courts her charmingly and wins her heart, but fails to make any impression on Dr. Sloper, who spots him for what he is. Her love for Morris gives Catherine the strength to stand against her father, who refuses to condone the marriage and tells her he will disinherit her if she goes ahead with it. She tells him that this makes little difference to her—but it makes a great deal of difference to Morris, who vanishes.

Catherine is shattered by the desertion and laments to her Aunt Lavinia (Miriam Hopkins), "Morris must love me, for all those who didn't." The despair eats into her heart, but when her father points out her folly, she responds coldly, "I don't know that Morris would have starved me for affection any more than you have." Much later, when her aunt remarks upon how cruel Catherine has become, she replies, "Yes, I can be very cruel. I have been taught by masters."

Despite his threat to disinherit her, Dr. Sloper leaves everything to her when he realizes that death is quickly approaching him through lung fever. Despite his plight, Catherine does not soften in her attitude toward her father and refuses to visit his death bed. Seven years pass, during which time Catherine matures into a more attractive and strong-minded woman. Her aunt tells her that Morris has returned and that he very much wants to see her. She agrees and appears to listen sympathetically when he explains his reasons for desertion. He did not, he pleads, want her to lose her inheritance on his behalf. Misled by her seemingly warm manner, he finds the courage to propose for the second time. Since they planned to elope on the first occasion, why not another elopement? Catherine tells him to return to the house later that night for her. He does—but to no avail. Morris bangs on the locked front door as Catherine sits in her parlor calmly finishing the embroidery that has been a lifetime hobby. Once she finishes this particular piece, she cuts the wool, never to embroider again. It is a symbol of a life that has gone. She lifts a lamp and walks the long flight upstairs as Morris beats in vain on the door and watches the light diminish in the house. Only moments before, Catherine had told her aunt, "He came twice—I shall see to it he never comes a third time." She is true to her word.

The Oscar was a just reward for an extraordinary piece of acting, certainly one of the finest ever realized by an actress on the screen. Olivia's Catherine Sloper is an illuminating study of a woman, ranging from an inhibited, passive innocent to an almost dominant, liberated lady. The metamorphosis is slow but exact as the texture of Catherine's personality changes. At first the eyes are those of someone cowed and begging for approval. By the end of the film the eyes are those of a woman who has not been crushed by the brutal treatment of the two men in her life. Hav-

With Ralph Richardson

220

ing rejected Morris and having put aside her embroidery forever, Catherine can look at herself and others with a cool, firm gaze. She is a survivor, she has not been crushed and she has achieved an inner peace that bodes well for the future.

Olivia's performance plays against Ralph Richardson's perfectly, as he projects the aloof, conceited iceberg of a father. She claims that it was a difficult film to make because of Richardson's behaving on the set much like the character he was playing. In her opinion he was an unsympathetic co-worker and worked all manner of tricks to steal the scenes. Olivia describes Richardson as a "wicked, selfish man." For all that, his playing of Dr. Sloper is precisely what the film needed, and it might be that his unpleasant behavior toward his co-star helped create the tension that works so well for their relationship on the screen.

The Heiress is a triumph in the film career of Olivia de Havilland, but it sadly marks the end of her short reign as a top flight, greatly respected actress. With this film, *The Snake Pit* and *To Each His Own,* all made in a three-year span, she had proved her command of the screen and the range of her talent. It was almost as if there was nothing left to prove— and she would allow three years to go by before making another picture. The pinnacle had been reached and it would never be quite the same again.

With Montgomery Clift and Miriam Hopkins

MY COUSIN RACHEL

1953
A 20th Century-Fox Picture,
Produced by Nunnally Johnson,
Directed by Henry Koster,
Written by Nunnally Johnson, based on the novel by Daphne du
   Maurier,
Photographed by Joseph La Shelle,
Music by Franz Waxman,
98 minutes.

CAST:

Rachel (Olivia de Havilland); *Philip Ashley* (Richard Burton); *Louise* (Audrey Dalton); *Nick Kendall* (Ronald Squire); *Rainaldi* (George Dolenz); *Ambrose Ashley* (John Sutton); *Seecombe* (Tudor Owen); *Reverend Pascoe* (J. M. Kerrigan); *Mrs. Pascoe* (Margaret Brewster); *Mary Pascoe* (Alma Lawton).

Three years after her triumph with *The Heiress*—a strangely long period for a successful actress to be away from the screen—Olivia de Havilland returned with a handsome film version of Daphne du Maurier's gothic romance *My Cousin Rachel*. It was an ideal vehicle on the face of it, allowing Olivia to resume her natural beauty after having played it down so much in *The Snake Pit* and *The Heiress*. Here she is again the elegant lady in gorgeous period costumes (shades of the Flynn swashbucklers), but unfortunately the role of Rachel is enigmatic and puzzling. To arrive at the end of a gothic novel and not know if the lady is innocent or guilty is perhaps intriguing. To come to the end of a film, having come to know her in the concentrated time span of two hours, and to be faced with the same puzzle is more annoying than intriguing. Possibly for this reason the film was less successful than its producers had hoped.

My Cousin Rachel was slated to be directed by George Cukor, who had hoped to use it as a means of enticing Greta Garbo back to the screen. When she refused, Cukor gladly turned to Olivia. He also persuaded Darryl F. Zanuck that the part of the young male lead should go to Richard Burton, who had appeared in a few British pictures of little impact but who had electrified audiences at the Old Vic with his playing of *Hamlet*. The fact that he seemed like a young Laurence Olivier and might possibly remind moviegoers of the wild, romantic Heathcliff of *Wuthering Heights* doubtlessly influenced Zanuck's thinking. In was, in fact, a successful Hollywood debut for Burton and won him a Fox contract. However, by the time Burton arrived for the job Cukor had withdrawn, due to dissatisfaction with the script and concept, and Henry Koster had been assigned as director, leaving the picture with another puzzle hanging over its head. Would it have been a greater film had it been directed by Cukor?

The setting is Cornwall in the early nineteenth century, with most of the action taking place in a magnificent mansion on the edge of the craggy, wave-swept coast with wild moors in the background. Philip Ashley (Burton) learns that his cousin Ambrose (John Sutton) has died under strange circumstances in Italy. Philip is shattered by the news because Ambrose was his benefactor and foster father. The last letters Philip had received from Ambrose intimated that he was being poisoned by his lovely young wife Rachel. When she arrives at the estate in Cornwall, she is greeted formally but coldly by Philip, who is nonetheless fascinated by her beauty, charm, and poise. Rachel has a mature sensuousness about her and Philip soon finds himself falling in love with her. When the will makes him the sole inheritor of the estate, Philip immediately grants her a generous annual allowance.

When Philip confronts Rachel with some of Ambrose's letters, which allude to the deceased guardian's fears about his life, Philip is satisfied with her explanation that the doctors advised her that Ambrose might react in a paranoid manner because of a brain tumor and gradual demetia. On his twenty-fifth birthday, now completely in love with Rachel, Philip turns over his estate to her, including the family jewels. In rapture he drapes the jewels around her neck and tells her of his devotion. However, suspicion seeps its way back into his thinking when Rachel's Italian lawyer Rainaldi (George Dolenz), a rather amorous fellow,

With Richard Burton

With George Dolenz and
Richard Burton

appears on the scene and suggests that he drink some of the herbal tea that Rachel brews. Philip does and becomes ill. Rachel nurses him through the sickness, during the course of which he hallucinates and imagines that he and Rachel have married. When well again, he realizes the sad truth and begs her to marry him. She refuses and in a fit of fury he attempts to strangle her, but manages to come to his senses before she chokes. His anger toward her is heightened by witnessing her apparent rendezvous with Rainaldi. Philip's former fiancee (Audrey Dalton) encourages him to be happy when Rachel announces she intends to leave. Now convinced that she actually murdered Ambrose, Philip lets Rachel go to almost certain death by failing to warn her about the unsafe condition of a wooden bridge on the cliffs. It collapses, Rachel falls to the rocks below, and dies in the arms of the distraught Philip, whose change of heart was not in time to save her. Having just read one of Rainaldi's notes to her, a note which proves Rachel's friendly relationship with him was based on business, poor Philip will forever be tormented by doubts. Was she a killer or an innocent victim of circumstances?

The question that plagues Philip as *My Cousin Rachel* draws to a close also plagues the viewer, too much so to be merely titillating. However, the movie has its compensations, chief of which is the pleasure of seeing Olivia again in a framework of classic elegance. The detailed black-and-white photography of Joseph La Shelle is a reminder of how dramatically effective that process could be in the right hands, and the sad-romantic score by Franz Waxman is a perfect subliminal commentary. It was Waxman who provided the beautiful score to Joan Fontaine's *Rebecca* (1939), which tends to underline the fact that Olivia's foray into Du Maurier territory was far less successful than sister Joan's.

With Audrey Dalton and Richard Burton

THAT LADY

1955
A 20th Century-Fox Picture,
Produced by Sy Bartlett,
Directed by Terence Young,
Written by Anthony Veiller and Sy Bartlett, based on a play by Kate O'Brien,
Photographed in De Luxe Color and CinemaScope by Robert Krasker,
Music by John Addison,
100 minutes.

CAST:

Ana de Mendoza (Olivia de Havilland); *Antonio Perez* (Gilbert Roland); *King Phillip II* (Paul Scofield); *Bernadina* (Francoise Rosay); *Mateo Vasquez* (Dennis Price); *Don Inigo* (Anthony Dawson); *Cardinal* (Robert Harris); *Diego* (Peter Illing); *Don Escoveda* (Jose Nieto); *Captain of the Guard* (Christopher Lee); *Fernando* (Andy Shine).

With Françoise Rosay

Another three-year absence from the screen and another return to historical romance, with lovely costumes and handsome sets, but sadly with little commercial impact. The very title of *That Lady* is so vague as to defy curiosity and as produced it is a film with little vitality. It also required another sad ending for Olivia de Havilland, this time as an actual historical figure—Ana de Mendoza, the one-eyed but beauteous Spanish princess who was the unrequited love of King Philip II, played by Paul Scofield in his film debut. This "love and death" saga of seventeenth century Spain had been a 1949 play on Broadway, starring Katharine Cornell, and it had turned out to be one of her less memorable vehicles. In turning it into a color movie made on location amid real Spanish courts and castles, the producers doubtlessly reckoned they would fare better. To have done so they would have needed less dialogue and more action.

Ana, also known as the Princess of Eboli, wears a black patch over her right eye, in which she was blinded as a youth when fighting a duel in defence of her king, the despotic Philip. Thereafter she and the monarch were close friends, although his passion for her was never consummated. She married one of Philip's ministers, bore him a son, and soon became a widow. Now Philip calls upon her to assist in coaching a commoner, Antonio Perez (Gilbert Roland), for the office of first secretary to the crown. The result is more than Philip bargained for as Ana and Antonio become lovers and create a scandal in court, always the scene of perpetual intrigue. Philip has Antonio arrested on a drummed-up charge of murder, and when Ana refuses to leave Madrid, she too is arrested. After spending time in jail, she is transferred to her home and held in check. Antonio escapes and makes his way to Ana, who persuades him to leave the country and take her son. Ana's health sinks with her spirits and after she receives a note from Antonio telling her that he and the boy are safe abroad, she dies. Her death grieves Philip, who realizes he has been too harsh.

The historical facts are fairly accurate but not presented with much flair. *That Lady* is at its best in moments of travelogue, as the color cameras capture vistas of Spanish landscape and splendid architecture. It also contains a well-staged bull fight, with Gilbert Roland dashing into the ring to heroically rescue a fallen matador. The film's major asset is the performance of Paul Scofield as the tormented Philip. Olivia's Ana is a warm account of a troubled and thwarted beauty, but the effort is sadly lost in this lumbering essay. It was said of Ana that even with only one eye she was more interesting than most women with two. Olivia manages to illustrate that point clearly.

With Gilbert Roland

With Paul Scofield, Gilbert Roland and Robert Harris

NOT AS A STRANGER

1955
A United Artists Release,
Produced and directed by Stanley Kramer,
Written by Edna and Edward Anhalt, based on the novel by Morton
Thompson,
Photographed by Franz Planer,
Music by George Antheil,
135 minutes.

CAST:

Kristina Hedvigson (Olivia de Havilland); *Lucas Marsh* (Robert Mitchum);
Alfred Boone (Frank Sinatra); *Harriet Lang* (Gloria Grahame); *Dr. Aarons*
(Broderick Crawford); *Dr. Runkleman* (Charles Bickford); *Dr. Snider*
(Myron McCormick); *Job Marsh* (Lon Chaney, Jr.); *Ben Cosgrove* (Jesse
White); *Oley* (Harry Morgan); *Brundage* (Lee Marvin); *Bruni* (Virginia
Christine); *Dr. Dietrich* (Whit Bissell); *Dr. Lettering* (Jack Raine); *Miss
O'Dell* (Mae Clarke).

For his debut as a director, after some years as a producer of films like
Champion (1949), *High Noon* (1952), and *Death of a Salesman* (1952),
Stanley Kramer chose to turn Morton Thompson's huge (almost one
thousand pages) best-seller, *Not as a Stranger,* into a movie. Kramer, then
and afterwards a man with a passion for strong issues, pulled no punches
in depicting life in the medical world. He backed Thompson's views that,
while medicine may be a noble profession, not all doctors are noble and
that business judgment sometimes overcomes ethics.

The fault most often levelled against Kramer is that of being over-
earnest in tackling controversial subjects and also of being short on humor. *Not as a Stranger* is a case in point. It is admirable in its almost docu-
mentary examination of medical standards and practices but becomes
tedious in probing into the private lives of its characters. In that regard it
was a challenge to Olivia de Havilland, because the part of the Swedish-
born nurse Kristina Hedwigson—complete with accent and platinum
blonde hair—was not, as written, very interesting and might, in less capable hands, have lapsed into caricature.

The central character is Lucas Marsh (Robert Mitchum), an intern
bent upon becoming a first-class doctor, not merely a successful one. He
courts and marries the warm-hearted Kristina, not out of love but because she is highly knowledgeable in the skills of the operating room and
because she has frugally put aside her savings through the years. She will

be, as he shrewdly knows, a supportive wife in every way. She helps make him the success he wants to be and cheerfully moves with him to the small town in which he starts his practice. But as much as he tries to be a good husband to the undemanding Kristina, Marsh easily falls into the arms of a local siren (Gloria Grahame) and the patience of the long-sorrowing Kristina wears thin. She reasons he no longer needs her and asks for a divorce. A calamity now brings Marsh to his senses. Dr. Runkleman (Charles Bickford), Marsh's gruff and wise employer, is stricken with a heart attack and requires emergency surgery. Marsh operates but makes a mistake, which costs Runkleman his life. Contrite in the realization that he has much to learn, Marsh returns to Kristina and tells her he needs her love, her guidance, and her understanding in order to make a success of his life. She is pleased to take him back.

Many critics pointed out that the laconic Mitchum was far *too* laconic in his playing of Marsh and thereby tended to make the part both dull and unsympathetic. Bickford won praise for his playing of the wise old Runkleman, as did Broderick Crawford as a tough teacher-pathologist and Frank Sinatra as a glib, money-happy internist. Olivia did fairly well by the critics, most of whom pointed out that Kristina was a bit too saintly to be believable. All were impressed with Kramer's realistic depiction of hospital life and scenes of surgery. In order to arrive at the greatest possible accuracy for his actors, Kramer required them to spend time in various hospitals in Los Angeles to observe methods and manners. Recalls Olivia, "I studied books on nursing and learned about operating techniques and terminology. But if I'd stopped there and assumed I then knew something about hospital life, it would have been like looking at the surface of the sea without being aware of the life that goes on underneath." Reportedly she would spend all day at a hospital while the film was in preparation and then go to the actors' rehearsals in the evening. A real nurse was overheard to say, "If that's a sample of the glamorous life of a movie star, she can have it."

With Frank Sinatra and Robert Mitchum

THE AMBASSADOR'S DAUGHTER

1956
A United Artists Release,
Produced and directed by Norman Krasna,
Written by Norman Krasna,
Photographed in De Luxe Color by Michael Kelber,
Music by Jacques Metchen,
102 minutes.

CAST:

Joan (Olivia de Havilland); *Danny* (John Forsythe); *Mrs. Cartwright* (Myrna Loy); *Senator Cartwright* (Adolphe Menjou); *Prince Nicholas* (Francis Lederer); *Ambassador Fiske* (Edward Arnold); *General Harvey* (Minor Watson); *Al* (Tommy Noonan).

With Edward Arnold

With Minor Watson, Edward Arnold, Adolphe Menjou and Myrna Loy

The Ambassador's Daughter was, apparently, an offer that Olivia de Havilland could not resist: a light-hearted comedy to be filmed in Technicolor in her new hometown, Paris, and concocted by writer-director-producer Norman Krasna, who had been responsible for her delightful *Princess O'Rourke* a dozen years previously. The title role called for a younger actress, but Olivia, on the verge of forty, here looks remarkably youthful. Her radiance must surely be due more than a little to her being the bride of magazine editor Pierre Galante and a welcome addition to Parisian society. This radiance, plus the excellent CinemaScope photography by Michael Kelber of the magnificent city, almost compensates for the rather weak scenario.

The lady of the title is Joan Fiske, the daughter of the American ambassador to France (Edward Arnold), who is visited by Senator Cartwright (Adolphe Menjou) and his wife (Myrna Loy). The senator has a bee in his bonnet. He believes that American servicemen are not giving Europeans a good impression because of their rowdy behavior and he suggests that Paris be put off-limits to them. U.S. Army General Harvey (Minor Watson) appeals to the ambassador to resist the senator's severe intentions and he brings in one of his men, a sergeant named Danny (John Forsythe), to show just how gentlemanly an American soldier can be. Danny meets Joan and falls in love with her, but does not know that she is the daughter of the ambassador. Because she wears clothes by Christian Dior, he assumes her to be a Dior model. Joan finds this amusing and togehter they have a good time as he escorts her around Paris.

However, this does not amuse her titled fiance (Francis Lederer), a hand-kissing, formal gent of the Old School. Mrs. Cartwright immediately senses that he is not the man for Joan and does her best to promote the affair with the sergeant. When Danny finds out who she is and why she has played a game with him, he is understandably vexed. She explains: For the sake of the American image, she made a bet with the senator that GIs were generally well behaved and civilized; she wanted to prove him wrong, as she has. Danny's behavior has won her the bet. It has also won him her heart, and, once he realizes this, all is well; the sergeant will likely become the ambassador's son-in-law.

Running too long and not sufficiently amusing to sustain itself, *The Ambassador's Daughter* is mere romantic froth and difficult to dislike. The real pleasure is in seeing Olivia so happy in such a nice setting, and getting a crack at comedy after so many searing dramas. A dozen years is a long time for even the best actress to go without having a few laughs on the screen.

With Francis Lederer

Both with John Forsythe

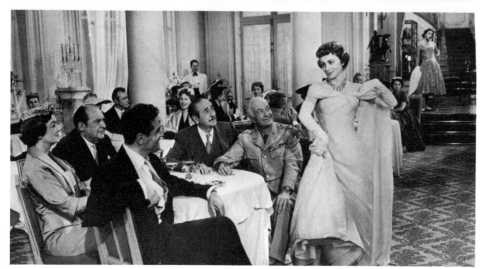

With Myrna Loy, Edward Arnold, Adolphe Menjou and Minor Watson

THE PROUD REBEL

1958
A Buena Vista Release,
Produced by Samuel Goldwyn, Jr.,
Directed by Michael Curtiz,
Written by Joseph Patracca and Lillie Hayward, based on a story by
 James Edward Grant,
Photographed in De Luxe Color by Ted McCord,
Music by Jerome Moross,
103 minutes.

CAST:

John Chandler (Alan Ladd); *Linnett Moore* (Olivia de Havilland); *Harry Burleigh* (Dean Jagger); *David Chandler* (David Ladd); *Dr. Enos Davis* (Cecil Kellaway); *Jeb Burleigh* (Dean Stanton); *Tom Burleigh* (Thomas Pittman); *Judge Morley* (Henry Hull); *Eli Mintz* (Gorman); *Birm Bates* (James Westerfield); *Salesman* (John Carradine).

Samuel Goldwyn, Jr., brought Olivia de Havilland back to Hollywood after a three-year absence to play opposite Alan Ladd in a picture he had been wanting to make for ten years. Goldwyn Jr. bought the James Edward Grant story from his father and planned its production for a long time before bringing it to life. *The Proud Rebel* is an unusually good western about a father-son relationship and noteworthy as one of Alan Ladd's most sensitive performances, a fact that surely stemmed from Ladd's having his own son David, then twelve, playing the boy in the picture. Goldwyn Jr. wanted Olivia for the female lead and she accepted as soon as she read the script. She also negotiated her own contract, which is the kind of forthright thing the no-nonsense lady in this particular story would have done. The role of Linnett Moore is that of a spinster who has held off marriage because she has never met the right man; she runs a farm all by herself, doing practically everything a man can do. In accepting the film Olivia was pleased to find that it reunited her with the veteran Michael Curtiz, whom she now found to be more mellow than in his halcyon days at Warners but still a director who kept a tight rein on his projects. *The Proud Rebel* needed his kind of discipline. In less firm hands this story of a mute boy and his love for his devoted father—and a devoted dog—might have slipped into self-defeating sentimentality.

The rebel of the title is an ex-Confederate soldier, John Chandler (Ladd), whose wife was killed in the battle of Atlanta, the witnessing of which caused their son David to lose the power of speech. After the war

Chandler journeys north in order to find a doctor who can cure the boy. With no funds, Chandler picks up work wherever he can. In Illinois he meets a Quaker doctor (Cecil Kellaway), who suggests that a colleague in Minnesota might be able to help. While Chandler tries to find work, two loutish young men, the sons of a scheming sheep raiser, Harry Burleigh (Dean Jagger), try to steal David's dog. Chandler fights them but is knocked unconscious by Burleight, who charges him with disturbing the peace and has him jailed. Linnett Moore, who refuses to sell her land to Burleigh, takes pity on the boy and pays Chandler's fine, and then hires him so that he can pay if off.

Chandler and David find solace with Linnett, who hides her feminine compassion behind a somewhat mannish exterior. The townspeople gossip about their living together. The success with which Linnett is now able to run her farm is shattered by the brutal Burleigh, who drives his sheep across her property, ruining the crops. Later he sets fire to her barn, doing everything he can to get her to give in, sell out, and move on. Chandler grows heartsick upon hearing other children refer to his son as a "dummy" and sells the dog in order to raise the money to visit the Minnesota doctor. The operation is a failure and David hates his father for having sold the dog, which has now, deliberately, been bought by Burleigh. Chandler tries to buy the dog back, but Burleigh's vicious attitude toward the dog and his refusal to return it triggers a gun fight in which the Burleighs meet their end. But it is the gunfight that proves to be salvation for Chandler and his son. At one point, when Burleigh is about to get the drop on Chandler, David yells a warning to save his father's life. With his voice returned and with Linnett deciding that she has finally found her man, life takes on new meaning for them all.

The film is greatly aided by the winning performance of David Ladd, whose father decided to accept the lead after coaching his son for his role. Several male stars has turned down the part because it was obviously a "boy and his dog" picture, two of the most feared up-staging factors in film-making. But as Ladd explained, "They say you don't have a chance against a boy or a dog, but after all, it's my boy." Olivia, on the other hand, had no need to worry about competing with either, since her role was that of the only woman in the picture, and a very strong woman at that. For *The Proud Rebel,* handsomely photographed in color on location in Utah, Olivia learned to hitch and drive a team of horses, do farm chores, handle a gun, and swing buckets of water to put out a fire. Having then mastered the art of being a tough frontier lady, she returned to the elegance of her home on the Right Bank in Paris.

With David Ladd

With Alan Ladd

With David and Alan Ladd

LIBEL

1959
An MGM Picture,
Produced by Anatole de Grunwald,
Directed by Anthony Asquith,
Written by Anatole de Grunwald and Karl Tunberg, based on the
  play by Edward Wooll,
Photographed by Robert Krasker,
Music by Benjamin Frankel,
100 minutes.

CAST:

Sir Mark Loddon/Frank Welney (Dirk Bogarde); *Lady Maggie Loddon* (Olivia de Havilland); *Jeffrey Buckenham* (Paul Massie); *Sir Wilfred* (Robert Morley); *Hubert Foxley* (Wilfrid Hyde-White); *Gerald Loddon* (Anthony Dawson); *Judge* (Richard Wattis); *Richard Dimbleby* (Himself); *Dr. Schrott* (Martin Miller); *Maisie* (Millicent Martin); *Guide* (Bill Shine); *Admiral Loddon* (Ivan Samson); *Michael Loddon* (Sebastian Saville); *Maddox* (Gordon Stern); *Mrs. Squires* (Josephine Middleton); *Fitch* (Kenneth Giffith); *Miss Sykes* (Joyce Carey).

Olivia de Havilland's next screen role could hardly have been more different from the hardy Linnett Moore of the frontier. In *Libel* she is the refined, elegant, American-born wife of an English baronet, living in one of those fabled stately homes whose owners have to allow tourists to peek around in them in order to help pay the taxes. While it is a role easily within Olivia's own personal range, it offers far less in the way of characterization than her previous film. Lady Maggie Lodden, the wife of Sir Mark (Dirk Bogarde), knows nothing of hardship, until some shocking drama comes into her life.

Libel was a successful London stage play of 1934. It was updated by scenarists Karl Tunberg and Anatole de Grunwald, but it is yet another of the many instances of theatre material failing to be as persuasive when transferred to the screen. The story gets underway when a Canadian commercial pilot (Paul Massie) sees a telecast in London of an interview with Sir Mark Lodden at his home. The Canadian is convinced that the baronet is a fraud, that he is actually a look-alike actor named Frank Welney. The Canadian, the baronet, and the actor were all prisoners in the same German camp during the war and escaped together. One of them disappeared during the escape. Was he Sir Mark or Welney? The tabloids have a field day with the Canadian's accusations and Lady

Maggie urges her husband to sue for libel and engage the distinguished barrister Sir Wilfred (Robert Morley).

The long-drawn-out case is made complex by the fact that Sir Mark himself is not quite sure of his identity. Injured in the war, he stutters on occasion and has difficulty remembering portions of his life. As the evidence sways back and forth in court, it begins to appear that Sir Mark is an imposter and the possible murderer of the missing baronet. Even his wife is convinced of his guilt and turns against him. She denounces him as a stranger who stole her love. Then a surprise witness is lead into court, a battered hulk of unknown identity, labelled "No. 15" in the institution where he lives. The sight of him shocks Sir Mark into remembering what happened on that flight from the German camp. The pitifully injured, brain-damaged man before him is Frank Welney, whom Sir Mark had to beat into unconsciousness when Welney tried to kill him in order to assume his identity. The envious Welney thereby hoped to escape his humble origins and gain access to a grander way of life. Lady Maggie is overjoyed at the revelation and resumes her love for her husband.

With Robert Morley

Libel is interesting but confusing and, finally, not very plausible. Dirk Bogarde's performances as the baronet, the actor, and the battered No. 15 merit applause for giving clarification to the various men as the story switches back and forth between the past and the present. Olivia, again gowned by Christian Dior, looks perfectly marvelous as Lady Maggie—to the manor born—but it is not a role which offered her much challenge or allows for much comment. We can only be happy for Sir Mark Lodden that she is there with him.

With Dirk Bogarde

LIGHT IN THE PIAZZA

1962
An MGM Picture,
Produced by Arthur Freed,
Directed by Guy Green,
Written by Julius J. Epstein, based on the novel by Elizabeth Spencer,
Photographed in De Luxe Color by Otto Heller,
Music by Mario Nascimbene,
101 minutes.

CAST:

Margaret Johnson (Olivia de Havilland); *Signor Naccarelli* (Rossano Brazzi); *Clara Johnson* (Yvette Mimieux); *Farazio Naccarelli* (George Hamilton); *Noel Johnson* (Barry Sullivan); *Miss Hawtree* (Isabel Dean); *The Minister* (Moultrie Kelsall); *Signora Naccarelli* (Nancy Nevinson).

Olivia de Havilland allowed another three years to drift by before accepting another film, and it is an indication of the esteem of her fellow professionals that she could maintain top billing under such conditions. With most stars almost desperately striving to keep in the public eye, she calmly took her time and her pick. What she picked next was a beautiful treatment by Julius Epstein of Elizabeth Spencer's novel *Light in the Piazza*, which dealt with mental retardation in a touching and romantic way. That the film was to be shot in color in Rome and Florence might have been a considerable factor in Olivia's deciding to do it. Indeed, the photography of the two handsome cities, particularly Florence, is stunning. Art lovers here have the chance to glimpse such delights as Michelangelo's statue of David and Cellini's *Perseus*, and for the first time ever motion picture cameras were allowed within the walls of the Uffizi Palace to film its treasury of masterpieces. All *that*, plus a good story told with taste and style.

The story is that of an attractive, American, middle-class matron, Margaret Johnson, who takes her twenty-six-year-old daughter Clara (Yvette Mimieux) on an extended trip to Italy in the hope that it may somehow put some spark in her life. Due to an accident at the age of ten, Clara has the mentality of that age. But she is charming, cheerful, and radiantly innocent, and her loving mother has to learn that she cannot be pushed beyond her mentality, that her brain has developed as far as it will ever go. The lovely Clara soon comes to the attention of a handsome young Florentine, Farazio Naccarelli (George Hamilton), who delights in her—and she in him. He asks her to marry him and she accepts, which meets with mixed emotions on the part of her mother. What Mother gradually has to understand is that Farazio is not much brighter than her daughter. In fact, since he comes from a solid, middle-class family and money is not a problem, and the young couple can have normal children, there seems little to worry about. The problem lies with the fathers. Margaret sends for her husband (Barry Sullivan), a rather shallow-hearted man, whose only suggestion is that their daughter be placed in an institution. Margaret clings to the hope that life has more to offer Clara than that. The father shrugs his shoulders and returns home. Signor Naccarelli (Rossano Brazzi) is harder to deal with, partly because he takes a flirtatious interest in Margaret, who knows that she must at least give him some understanding of the problem. She manages to do that, and as the happy couple leave the church after their wedding, she muses, "I did the right thing. I know I did."

Olivia certainly did the right thing in agreeing to star in this exquisite movie, which deftly combines a travelogue with a modern problem play and balances American common sense with the more sanguine Italian view of life. Her portrait of the mother, a genuinely loving human being trying to do the best for her daughter while holding on to her marriage and her own right to happiness, is yet another highlight in Olivia's gallery of various kinds of women. This one, hiding her anxieties behind a happy facade and never lacking the courage of her convictions, would be welcome anywhere. It is a performance of great consistency and subtle projection, and only occasionally does the actress let the audience glimpse into the shadows of Margaret Johnson's mind, to see the worried mother behind the serene lady. When she says, "Every mother, in some way, wants a little girl who never grows up," Olivia conveys the feeling that the mother doesn't really believe what she is saying. Hers is a touching, poignant dilemma; but hers is also the final victory. Margaret Johnson's plan to take Clara to Italy and perhaps open up a new world to the girl is a success. She does indeed find some light in the piazza.

With Rossano Brazzi

LADY IN A CAGE

1964
A Paramount Picture,
Produced by Luther Davis,
Directed by Walter Grauman,
Written by Luther Davis,
Photographed by Lee Garmes,
100 minutes.

CAST:

Mrs. Hilyard (Olivia de Havilland); *Sade* (Ann Sothern); *The Wino* (Jeff Corey); *Randall* (James Caan); *Elaine* (Jennifer Billingsley); *Essie* (Rafael Campos); *Malcolm Hilyard* (William Swan); *Junkyard Proprietor* (Charles Seel); *Assistant Junkman* (Scatman Crothers).

Lady in a Cage is the only controversial film in which Olivia de Havilland has appeared. In England it was banned for its violence and in American it met with mostly tepid reviews. Many wondered why such a cultured actress would appear in such searing material, to which Olivia replied that she believed the film said something valid about the crime situation in large, modern cities. During the promotional tour she made for the picture she also admitted that she owned a share of its profits. "Perhaps it was two or three years ahead of its time. I think some day it will be recognized as a depiction of the aimless violence of our era."

With James Caan

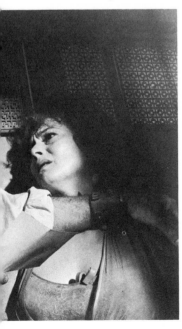

The lady is Mrs. Hilyard, a wealthy poetesss who lives in a three-story city mansion and her cage is her elevator, which jams a dozen feet short of the main floor due to an electrical failure. She rings her outside alarm, but this is a July 4th weekend and there is too much traffic and commotion in the street for anyone to notice. Mrs. Hilyard is using her elevator because she is recovering from a hip injury. She is also in a state of emotional turmoil because her twenty-nine-year-old son (William Swan) has finally rebelled against her domineering, smothering mother love. The turmoil soon turns into panic. Eventually her alarm is noticed by a drunken derelict (Jeff Corey), who breaks into the house, ignores her plight and helps himself to various fixtures and alcohol. He leaves with his loot but returns a while later with a plumb prostitute (Ann Sothern) and three teenage hooligans, who proceed to terrorize Mrs. Hilyard as they wreck her home.

Randall (James Caan), the leader of the group, is a psychotic and delights in tormenting the lady in the cage. She pleads to be freed from the elevator and tells them they can have anything if they will only help her. This serves only to intensify their frenzy of destruction. When her bribes fail she shrieks in despair, "You are so much of that offal of the Welfare State! You are what my tax money goes for" Things get worse and worse, as the hoodlums murder the drunk with a switchblade and lock the prostitute in the wine cellar. Mrs. Hilyard manages to open the door of the elevator and makes a painful jump to the floor. While in the elevator she has torn off two small strips of metal and she uses these to plunge into Randall's eyes. His cohorts flee at this bloody turn of events and she drags herself out through the front door onto the sidewalk. The blinded Randall tries to stop her but he stumbles into the street and is run over by a car. Finally, lying on the sidewalk and screaming for help, Mrs. Hilyard receives the attention of passersby.

Producer-writer Luther Davis was defensive about the rough reception afforded *Lady in a Cage* by the critics. He claimed that it was based on material he knew to be true and that he had made the film to shock the public into realizing the danger and depravity that now ravaged American cities and the indifference shown by fellow citizens. The critics claimed that he had overstated his case and allowed the film to become a horrible display of violence and gore, an indulgence in mayhem that defeated its own purpose.

Olivia's performance as Mrs. Hilyard is admirable in its execution but uncomfortable, especially for her admirers, to watch. She spares no detail in sketching the character of a women of great refinement who is reduced by fear and hysteria to an almost animal level. But her plight is somewhat reduced for the audience by the fact that Mrs. Hilyard is a less than sympathetic character. She admits to herself that her abnormal love for her son has blighted him and she confesses, "It's all true. I am a monster." *Lady in a Cage* might have made better points if the lady had been kinder and had the producer and director not made the horror quite so graphic. Nonetheless, the British magazine *Films and Filming* selected her performance as the best given by an actress in 1964. *Time,* on the other hand, was less generous and thought the film's only virtue was that it gave Olivia "a chance to go ape." The question is. Who wants to see a lady going ape?

HUSH . . . HUSH, SWEET CHARLOTTE

1964
A 20th Century-Fox Picture,
Produced and directed by Robert Aldrich,
Written by Henry Farrell and Lukas Heller,
Photographed by Joseph Biroc,
Music by Frank De Vol,
133 minutes.

CAST:

Charlotte Hollis (Bette Davis); *Miriam Deering* (Olivia de Havilland); *Dr. Drew Bayliss* (Joseph Cotten); *Velma Cruther* (Agnes Moorehead); *Harry Willis* (Cecil Kellaway); *Big Sam Hollis* (Victor Buono); *Jewel Mayhew* (Mary Astor); *Paul Marchand* (William Campbell); *Sheriff Luke Standish* (Wesley Addy); *John Mayhew* (Bruce Dern); *Taxi driver* (Dave Willock); *Foreman* (George Kennedy).

What Ever Happened to Baby Jane? (1962) revitalized the sagging careers of both Bette Davis and Joan Crawford by plunging them into the world of the grotesque. In the general Hollywood view, the former movie queens had reached the age where they were uncastable as leading ladies and now usable only as star cameo players. Producer-director Robert Aldrich thought otherwise and came up with the *Baby Jane* project, the success of which made Davis and Crawford instant *grandes dames de grand guignol.* Some kind of sequel bringing them together in a similarly styled horror outing became inevitable but it took two years for Aldrich to come up with one that pleased the two veterans, neither of whom really liked each other. But by the time *Hush. . . Hush, Sweet Charlotte* was ready for production, Crawford became ill and a replacement was needed. Aldrich wanted Loretta Young, but that dignified lady had no desire to be seen in a macabre picture. Bette Davis opted for her friend Olivia de Havilland and persuaded Aldrich to fly to Europe and try to talk her into the role. Davis knew it would take some persuasion. Like Loretta, Olivia had no particular desire to appear in the horror *genre* and she refused the part.

In the original script, the role of Miriam Deering is that of a harsh, crude, conniving woman. The shrewd Aldrich offered to change the concept of the role, keeping the vital conniving aspect but changing the image to that of a refined and charming and apparently sympathetic lady. This gave the character an ambivalence that no actress could resist.

Now intrigued with the role and pleased to be appearing on the screen again with Davis, Olivia became enthusiastic and told Hollywood reporter Bob Thomas that she loved the idea of a house full of intrigue and weird characters and crystal chandeliers. "The whole script fairly drips with Spanish moss. And it will be marvelous to work with Bette again. She is the only true genius we have had among the motion picture actresses."

Charlotte Hollis is anything but sweet. She is an aging spinster gradually sinking into dementia in her Louisiana mansion and haunted by horrible memories. Thirty-seven years ago her lover (Bruce Dern) was murdered in a horrible fashion, including the disappearance of his head, and the crime was never solved. Charlotte has always suspected that her father (Victor Buono) was responsible and that he had hidden the head somewhere in the house. With her home slated for demolition in order to make way for a highway, Charlotte fears that the hideous pieces of evidence will be discovered. She invites her cousin Miriam to come and stay with her and persuade the Highway Commission to change their plans.

Miriam soothes "sweet Charlotte" and tells her to "hush. . .hush." Everything will be all right. Everything is, of course, far from all right. That same night Charlotte awakens to hear a harpsichord playing a lullaby she used to know as a child, and when she creeps into the music room she finds a human head on the floor. Miriam brings in Dr. Drew Bayliss (Joseph Cotten) to treat Charlotte. The doctor is well aware of the family background; in fact, he and Miriam were engaged to be married thirty-seven years ago but he changed his mind in the aftermath of the scandal. Now Bayliss has changed his mind again. He has not only resumed his romance with Miriam but the two of them are in cahoots to drive Charlotte insane and gain control of her estate. Their plotting is overheard by Charlotte's housekeeper, Velma (Agnes Moorehead). She accuses Miriam of being a fortune hunter and is immediately dismissed by the doctor as an evil influence on Charlotte. Velma relates her suspicions to an insurance investigator (Cecil Kellaway), but she is killed by Miriam when she sneaks back into the house to warn the heavily drugged Charlotte.

Miriam's next device is to convince Charlotte that Dr. Bayliss has been murdered. Who killed him? Miriam sorrowfully tells her that she, poor, sweet Charlotte, did it and that together they must dispose of the body so that no one will ever know. They drive out to the swamps and dump the body, but when they get back to the mansion, the bloody, muddy corpse of the doctor stands on the staircase and smiles at Charlotte, who lapses into hysteria and then faints. Later she emerges from a long, drugged sleep and wanders out on her balcony. She looks down and spots Miriam and Bayliss in each other's arms and congratulating themselves on the success of their scheme. Charlotte pushes a huge, concrete flower vase onto the lovers and kills them.

The following morning, when Charlotte is taken into custody by the

With Agnes Moorehead

With Bette Davis

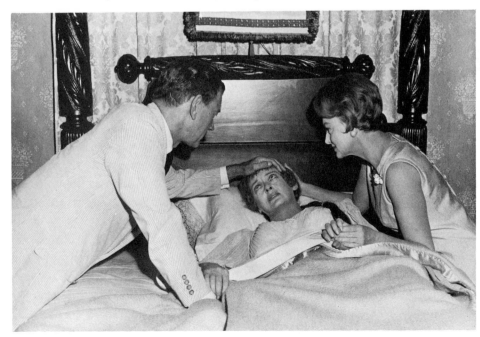

*With Joseph Cotten and
Bette Davis*

police, she is handed a letter by the insurance investigator. It clears up the mystery. Written by the recently deceased Jewel Maythew (Mary Astor), the estranged wife of the man Charlotte was going to marry long ago, it reveals that Jewel killed him and has been paying Miriam, who was a witness, to keep silent all through the years. Sweet Charlotte finally has the satisfaction of the truth and the comfort of knowing she is not mad.

Running way over two hours, *Hush. . . Hush, Sweet Charlotte* gave its customers—at least those with a taste for gothic horror—their money's worth. The ornate, decaying sourthern mansion made a fitting background for the macabre happenings, many of them far from being either logical or convincing; but the film's major impact is the bravura performance of Bette Davis. Again it is a florid and often ranting performance, and again it is Olivia who provides the perfect counterbalance with her quiet, restrained manner. But here the restraint and the charm are a mask for a truly evil woman, full of cunning and greed. It is a subtle piece of acting, with only a hint here and there of Miriam's motives beneath the polished, cultured surface. As such it is a vital contribution to the effectiveness of the film.

Recalls Olivia, "*Hush. . . Hush, Sweet Charlotte* was full of traps, it was a delicate tight-rope walking assignment. I found that very interesting. Aldrich gave it a very special style, a kind of dark glittering style which fascinated me." Changing the role of Miriam from the original concept of her as a rude woman to a polite and cultured lady gave Olivia her key to the performance. "It's always the charming ones of evil intent who are the dangerous ones; the others you can see coming. But you can't see Miriam coming, and she's really dangerous."

THE ADVENTURERS

1970
A Paramount Picture,
Produced and directed by Lewis Gilbert,
Written by Michael Hastings and Lewis Gilbert, based on the novel
  by Harold Robbins,
Photographed in De Luxe Color by Claude Renoir,
Music by Antonio Carlos Jobim,
171 minutes.

With Rossano Brazzi

CAST:

Dax Xenos (Bekim Fehmiu); *Rojo* (Alan Badel); *Sue Ann Daley* (Candice Bergen); *Fat Cat* (Ernest Borgnine); *Amparo* (Leigh Taylor-Young); *Jaime Xenos* (Fernando Rey); *Sergei Nikovitch* (Thommy Berggren); *Marcel Campion* (Charles Aznavour); *Deborah Hadley* (Olivia de Havilland); *Mr. Hadley* (John Ireland); *Caroline de Coyne* (Delia Boccardo); *Col. Guttierrez* (Sidney Tafler); *Baron de Coyne* (Rossano Brazzi); *Dania Leonardi* (Anna Moffo); *Robert* (Christian Roberts); *El Lobo* (Yorgo Voyagis); *El Condor* (Jorge Martinez de Hoyos); *Denisonde* (Angela Scoular).

Despite their vast popularity, the novels of Harold Robbins seldom translate to the screen with any great success. It seems that what is intriguingly trashy on the printed page becomes less intriguing when projected visually. Paramount's expensive treatment of *The Adventurers* would seem to prove the point. It lumbers on for almost three hours, to tell a convoluted tale of people who are brutal, greedy, over-sexed, treacherous, and selfish. And for reasons which now seem incomprehensible, Paramount risked this whole, vast venture by giving the leading role to a young Yugoslav actor, Bekim Fehmiu, of little charisma, looks, or acting ability.

The Adventurers began a new stage in Olivia de Havilland's screen career. Five years after her last film, she now returned as a "cameo" star, no longer in demand as a leading player but, because of her prestige and ability, always in demand to populate a picture with famous names. In the Robbins story she is Deborah Hadley, a wealthy American living in Rome, not very happily married and susceptible to romance. A young South American named Dax Zenos (Fehmiu) woos her because he needs money, but when he is finished with her and takes up with a young girl, Deborah has enough dignity not to try and hold on to him.

Dax is the product of revolution. As a boy he sees bandits pillage his home and kill his mother. His father, Jaime (Fernando Rey), joins the forces of a rebel leader, Rojo (Alan Badel). When Rojo gains control of

242

With Bekin Fehmiu, Candice Bergen and Rossana Brazzi

their country, Corteguay, he appoints Jaime as ambassador to Italy, where young Dax grows up amid high society and political intrigue, and much romancing. Jaime returns to Corteguay to find Rojo a brutal dictator, and when he moves to alter that situation, Rojo has him killed. Back in Rome without funds, Dax becomes a gigolo and at one point manages to get five thousand dollars out of Deborah Hadley. He then romances and marries the rich Sue Ann Daley (Candice Bergen) but divorces her when she is injured in an accident. Another revolution swells up in Corteguay and Dax decides to become part of the plan to overthrow Rojo. After a variety of adventures and some more romance, Dax kills Rojo but later loses his own life at the hands of another political fanatic.

The Adventurers was a flop, particularly in the opinion of film critics everywhere, who were appalled by its obvious leanings on sex and violence. Olivia emerged almost unscathed, with views ranging from the London *Observer*'s Dilys Powell saying that Olivia in this picture gave everyone a lesson in acting, to *Variety*'s terse comment that her appearance in the film is an embarrassment. *The Village Voice* hit a nice middle note by saying that she performed in this fetid epic "with a naturalness and with consideration for the audience's sentimental fondness for her." In short, she is the only touch of class in a shabby enterprise.

POPE JOAN

1972
A Big City Picture, released by Columbia-Warner,
Produced by Kurt Unger,
Directed by Michael Anderson,
Written by John Briley,
Photographed in Eastman Color by Billy Williams,
Music by Maurice Jarre,
132 minutes.

CAST:

Joan (Liv Ullmann); *Mother Superior* (Olivia de Havilland); *Cecilia* (Lesley-Anne Down); *Pope Leo* (Trevor Howard); *Joan's Father* (Jeremy Kemp); *Elder Monk* (Patrick Magee); *Louis* (Franco Nero); *Adrian* (Maximilian Schell); *Joan's Mother* (Natasha Nicolescu); *Young Joan* (Sharon Winter); *Emperor Louis* (Andre Morell); *Dr. Stevens* (Keir Dullea).

The least successful film in which Olivia de Havilland has appeared is *Pope Joan,* a European-made historical drama that did little business in Europe and has never received distribution in the United States. When shown to the press in New York, it received brutal reviews, mostly of the sarcastic kind, including a comment from Rex Reed that it was a demented exercise in religious hysteria. The film takes as its basis the possibility that there may have been a female pope in the ninth century, a dubious notion that has always been offensive to the Vatican. Although *Pope Joan* is an expensive, lavish spectacle, with many fine and famous performers, it is difficult to imagine its violence and sexual content not offending the Catholic Church.

Much of the film takes place in medieval Germany, but it sets up its story in the present as an American girl, Joan (Liv Ullmann), seeks advice from her analyst (Keir Dullea) about her obsession with the woman who may have been a pope. She believes she was that woman in a previous life and feels all her sufferings. In order to understand what she is talking about, the audience is transported back a thousand years. Medieval Joan is the daughter of a lusty minister (Jeremy Kemp) whose licentious nature is shared by his colleagues, who rape Joan when her father dies. Her intellect and her sexuality fascinate men and cause her perpetual turmoil. She seeks protection in a convent, where the kindly abbess (Olivia), impressed with her intelligence, gives her the job of librarian. The Roman Emperor (Andre Morell) pays a visit and his son Louis (Franco Nero) is smitten with Joan, who nonetheless rejects him. Later she gives in to the physical side of her nature and becomes the mistress of a monk, Adrian (Maximilian Schell). When the emperor dies the populace runs amok and sacks the convent, raping the nuns and crucifying the abbess. Joan escapes with Adrian, cuts her hair, dons the habit of a monk, and pretends to be a man named John. In Rome she impresses Pope Leo (Trevor Howard) with her ability as a preacher and he hires her as his private secretary. Her political advice is a so sage that with his coming death he nominates her as his successor, still not knowing she is a woman. Louis, now emperor-elect, is among those who believe Joan-John is not qualiied for the job and he moves his forces on Rome to oust the nominee. She threatens to excommunicate him and he then changes his mind and allows her to crown him. Later that night he discovers her true identity and makes love to her, causing a pregnancy which reveals her sex to the public, who turn on her and kill her.

Perhaps the material is too controversial ever to make an acceptable film. Certainly this version is too spicy for its own good, and it is a pity to see its many fine actors wallowing in medieval mire. Olivia makes the most of her scenes as the compassionate, dignified abbess, but the sight of her being crucified is hard to take.

With Liv Ullmann

246

AIRPORT '77

1977
A Universal Picture,
Produced by William Frye,
Executive producer: Jennings Lang,
Directed by Jerry Jameson,
Written by David Spector and Michael Scheff,
Photographed in De Luxe Color by Philip Lathrop,
Music by John Cacavas,
113 minutes.

CAST:

Don Gallagher (Jack Lemmon); *Karen Wallace* (Lee Grant); *Eve Clayton* (Brenda Vaccaro); *Nicholas St. Downs, III* (Joseph Cotten); *Emily Livingston* (Olivia de Havilland); *Buchek* (Darren McGavin); *Martin Wallace* (Christopher Lee); *Chambers* (Robert Foxworth); *Eddie* (Robert Hooks); *Patrone* (George Kennedy); *Stevens* (James Stewart); *Banker* (Monte Markham); *Julie* (Kathleen Quinlan); *Frank Powers* (Gil Gerrard); *Ralph Crawford* (James Booth); *Anne* (Monica Lewis); *Dorothy* (Maidie Norman); *Lisa* (Pamela Bellwood); *Mrs. Tern* (Arlene Golonka); *Lucas* (George Furth); *Commander Guay* (Richard Vanture).

Airport '77 equalled the success of *Airport '75*, which had been a follow-up to *Airport* (1970), an all-star-cast depiction of Arthur Hailey's best-selling novel. Little remained of Hailey's imprint in the third picture, other than his grand-hotel-of-the-air-in-danger concept. Here the danger is indeed frightening. A 747 airliner crash lands on the ocean and sinks in about 50 feet of water, while remaining intact and taking on the characteristics of a stricken submarine. The survival of the passengers becomes a race against time as the air quality diminishes and the fuselage of the huge airplane gradually shows strain and water begins to seep in.

Olivia de Havilland is Emily Livingston, a wealthy, matronly art patroness, who is one of the guests aboard the customized 747 belonging to a billionaire (James Stewart) who is transferring part of his vast art collection from New York to his estate in Florida. A team of meticulously prepared hijackers board the plane and shortly after it is airborne take it over, with the object of flying it to a Caribbean island, transferring the art collection to their own plane, and disappearing with it. To avoid radar detection they fly just above sea level, and while passing through fog banks the tip of one of the wings hits an oil derrick and they lose control of the plane. After it has sunk to the ocean floor, the proper pilot (Jack

Lemmon) resumes command. He manages to escape the plane, float to the surface, and attract the attention of a Coast Guard helicopter, which has been searching for the plane. The Navy then moves in with a team of frogmen, who place air balloons around the body of the 747 and bring it to the surface—at least soon enough to save the almost exhausted passengers.

Like its predecessors, *Airport '77* is at its best when dealing with the technical aspects of its story. The special effects are excellent and the rescue operation by the Navy is spectacularly interesting. The long film wavers when telling the stories of its many characters, which it does with both in-flight encounters and flashbacks. In reviewing the film for the *Los Angeles Times,* Charles Champlin observed, "It is a character list that could have been tailored and cast by computer or one of those spin-the-needle plot constructors once advertised in the back pages of pulp magazines. The delineations are paper thin and done in poster color, but with no pretense of being other than popular art."

Olivia emerges from *Airport '77* as one of the more admirable characters, although perhaps just a little too good-natured to be credible. Her Emily is a lady who sponsors young artists, loves to play poker (and usually wins), but who has been unlucky in love and sadly refers to three failed marriages. Once on board she comes across an old friend (Joseph Cotten), a man who once meant a great deal to her when she was a youngster but whom she has not seen since. Now that he is a widower, as well as an art connoisseur and financial adviser, it is reasonable to assume that he and Emily will find happiness together at this comfortable time in their lives.

For its actors, *Airport '77* contained some scenes of considerable discomfort, particularly the scene where the 747 begins to break up and water cascades over the survivors. To achieve this frightening moment, two huge drums, each containing two thousand gallons of water, were dumped on the set. Brenda Vaccaro contacted pneumonia as a result, but Olivia claims that all she lost in the drenching was an eyelash.

With Joseph Cotten

With Jack Lemmon and
Kathleen Quinlan

With Maidie Norman

THE FIFTH MUSKETEER

1977
A Sascha (Wien) Production, released by Columbia Pictures,
Produced by Ted Richmond,
Directed by Ken Annakin,
Written by Davis Ambrose, based on the novel *The Man in the Iron
    Mask* by Alexandre Dumas, and a screenplay by George Bruce,
Photographed in color by Jack Cardiff,
Music by Riz Ortolani,
103 minutes.

CAST:

King Louis XIV/Philippe (Beau Bridges); *Maria Theresa* (Sylvia Kristel);
Madame de la Valliere (Ursula Andress); *D'Artagnan* (Cornel Wilde);
Fouquet (Ian McShane); *Aramis* (Lloyd Bridges); *Porthos* (Alan Hale, Jr.);
Spanish Ambassador (Helmut Dantine); *Athos* (Jose Ferrer); *Colbert* (Rex
Harrison); *Queen Anne* (Olivia de Havilland).

Enthusiasts of the swashbuckling *genre,* particularly those of the
Alexandre Dumas branch, were much disappointed in *The Fifth Musketeer.* Filmed with a cast of veterans and utilizing superb Austrian scenery
and castles, the impressive parts somehow do not add up to an impressive
total. The film claims to have been based not only on Dumas but also on a
screenplay by George Bruce, but does not specify which was the major
influence. *The Fifth Musketeer* is virtually a remake of the 1939 *The Man in
the Iron Mask,* finely scripted by Bruce and stylishly directed by James
Whale. In that version Louis Hayward played King Louis XIV and his
twin brother Philippe, Joan Bennett was Maria Theresa, Warren William
was D'Artagnan, and Joseph Schildkraut was the villainous man-behind-
the-throne, Fouquet. The small role of Queen Anne, the mother of the
twins, was played by Doris Kenyon in 1939, and by Olivia de Havilland in
this strangely lacklustre version.

According to Dumas, Louis XIV (Beau Bridges) has an identical twin,
Philippe (also Bridges), who was separated from him at birth to avoid
later confusion about rights to the throne. It was a bad choice. Louis
turned out to be a petty; stupid man. According to this screenplay, the
wily, ambitious Fouquet (Ian McShane) sees his opportunity to gain control of France. He discovers that Philippe is alive and well, and persuades
him to substitute for the King, for the good of France. It is also his intention to then have Philippe assassinated. This evil plan comes to the attention of D'Artagnan (Cornel Wilde) and the musketeers: Aramis (Lloyd

Bridges), Porthos (Alan Hale, Jr.) and Athos (Jose Ferrer), all of whom have been friends of Philippe since his infancy.

Masquerading as the King, Philippe meets the King's bride-to-be, the lovely Spanish princess Maria Theresa (Sylvia Kristel) and falls in love with her. The attempted assassination is foiled by the loyal old minister Colbert (Rex Harrison), but Philippe is captured and imprisoned in the Bastille, with a mask over his face so that no one will recognize him. Colbert sends for D'Artagnan and the Musketeers, who fight their way into the Bastille and rescue Philippe. They rush Philippe to Notre Dame, where Louis is about to marry Maria Theresa and substitute him for the King. Queen Anne identifies Philippe as the rightful heir to the throne and Fouquet meets his end dueling with D'Artagnan.

The Fifth Musketeer was filmed under the title *Behind the Iron Mask* but Columbia changed it, presumably to cash in on Richard Lester's successful *The Three* (and the *Four*) *Musketeers*. To no avail. The film received very limited release in the United States, where critics pointed out that the sound quality of the dubbing was conspicuously bad and even Jack Cardiff's beautiful color photography did not atone for the tiredness of the acting and the lack of *élan* so necessary in this kind of picture. Most felt that its best features were the contributions of the veterans, especially sixty-year-old Cornel Wilde, in spirited fettle as the still dashing D'Artagnan, and seventy-year-old Rex Harrison as the wise Colbert. As for Olivia, her Queen Anne is gentle, sensitive, and elegant. A regal cameo indeed. What a pity *The fifth Musketeer* is not a better showcase.

Lloyd Bridges, Cornel Wilde, Alan Hale, Jr., and José Ferrer

THE SWARM

1978
A Warner Bros. Picture,
Produced and directed by Irwin Allen,
Written by Stirling Silliphant, based on the novel by Arthur Herzog,
Photographed in Panavision and Technicolor by Fred J.
  Koenekamp,
Music by Jerry Goldsmith,
116 minutes.

CAST:

Brad Crane (Michael Caine); *Helena* (Katharine Ross); *General Slater* (Richard Widmark); *Dr. Hubbard* (Richard Chamberlain); *Maureen Schuster* (Olivia de Havilland); *Felix* (Ben Johnson); *Anne MacGregor* (Lee Grant); *Dr. Andrews* (Jose Ferrer); *Rita Bard* (Patty Duke Astin); *Jud Hawkins* (Slim Pickens); *Major Baker* (Bradford Dillman); *Clarence* (Fred MacMurray); *Dr. Krim* (Henry Fonda); *General Thompson* (Cameron Mitchell); *Paul Durant* (Christian Juttner); *Dr. Newman* (Morgan Paull); *Dr. Martinez* (Alejandro Rey); *Pete Harris* (Don "Red" Barry); *Mrs. Durant* (Doria Cook); *Mr. Durant* (Robert Varney).

One of the phenomena of Hollywood during the Seventies was the emergence of the *disaster* film, films dealing with perils and catastrophes, such as sinking ships, crashing airplanes, rampaging diseases, and all forms of destructive weather. In a world fraught with actual disaster, movie audiences seemed to enjoy revelling in vicarious participation. No film producer has been more aware of this than Irwin Allen, whose tastes in film making have always leaned toward the bizarre (*The Lost World, Voyage to the Bottom of the Sea, Five Weeks in a Balloon,* etc.) and who delighted his investors by turning out two highly successful disaster items in *The Poseidon Adventure* (1972) and *The Towering Inferno* (1974). With the listing of disaster subjects rapidly being diminished by other producers, Allen next turned to the possibilities of humans being ravaged by killer bees. His policy in making this kind of film is to graphically present frightening situations and to populate them with as many famous faces as possible. In *The Swarm* he uses stars as character players to a greater extent than ever before. It boasts five Oscar winners, including Olivia de Havilland.

The story: Swarms of killer bees from South America invade southeast Texas and settle on a military base near Houston. An entomologist (Michael Caine), who has been tracking the swarm, is brought in to supervise the situation, to the disgust of General Slater (Richard Widmark), who would prefer to use purely military tactics to kill the invaders. When some people are killed by the bees, their children lead a revenge raid on the bees and cause the situation to become worse. The bees attack the nearby town of Marysville and kill several hundred people, including some school children. The principal, Maureen Schuster (Olivia), takes precautions which save many of her students, and she is in turn fussed over by her two suitors, the mayor (Fred MacMurray) and a retired engineer (Ben Johnson). Marysville is evacuated but many of the people are killed—including Maureen—when the train on which they depart is invaded by the bees, causing it to go out of control and crash. Houston is ruined by the bees, and all attempts to check them seem to be ineffective, until the entomologist discovers that the warning system of the military base puts out a signal that uses the same sound pattern as the Bees' mating call. The bees are then lured to a stretch of ocean sprayed with oil and subsequently incinerated.

Despite its potential as a particularly frightening kind of disaster caper, *The Swarm* did not impress audiences very much. The critics thought it

With Michael Caine, Katherine Ross and Irwin Allen

slack in narrative and far from convincing. Like most of the star players, Olivia found the film fascinating to work on because of its subject matter but nothing of a challenge on the acting level. In speaking of Irwin Allen, she says, "This is something he's very good at. He knows how to put a film of this kind together. He also has a very sensitive ear and a sensitive eye, so that in scenes which have nothing to do with the broad extravaganza effects, which are very theatrical and dramatic, he shows tremendous insight into personal relationships."

As of this writing (late 1980), *The Swarm* is the last film in which Olivia de Havilland has appeared. Since she is a lady of vitality, curiosity, good health, and willingness to work, it is reasonable to assume there will be other films. It would be a pity if there were not.

Hermia, Arabella Bishop, Maid Marian, Melanie Hamilton, Elizabeth Bacon Custer, Jody Norris, Virginia Cunningham, Catherine Sloper, even the beastly Terry of *The Dark Mirror*. . . they are all indelible, distinct images created by the talent of a remarkable actress, whose own image is indelible and distinct. And beautiful.

And finally, a reminder of a fondly remembered de Havilland image—Maid Marian and her Robin.